REVIEWS OF OTHER BOOKS BY RICHARD BLAKE

"Fascinating to read, very well written, an intriguing plot
and I enjoyed it very much."
(Derek Jacobi, star of *I Claudius* and *Gladiator*)

"Vivid characters, devious plotting and buckets of gore
are enhanced by his unfamiliar choice of period. Nasty,
fun and educational."
(*The Daily Telegraph*)

"He knows how to deliver a fast-paced story
and his grasp of the period is impressively detailed."
(*The Mail on Sunday*)

"A rollicking and raunchy read . . . Anyone who enjoys
their history with large dollops of action, sex, intrigue
and, above all, fun will absolutely love this novel."
(*Historical Novels*)

"As always, [his] plotting is as brilliantly devious as the
mind of his sardonic and very earthy hero. This is a story
of villainy that reels you in from its prosaic opening
through a series of death-defying thrills and spills."
(*The Lancashire Evening Post*)

"It would be hard to over-praise this extraordinary series,
a near-perfect blend of historical detail and atmosphere
with the plot of a conspiracy thriller, vivid characters,
high philosophy and vulgar comedy."
(*The Morning Star*)

Also by Richard Blake

Conspiracies of Rome
Terror of Constantinople
Blood of Alexandria
Sword of Damascus
Ghosts of Athens
Curse of Babylon

Writing as Sean Gabb

The Column of Phocas
The Churchill Memorandum
The Break
The York Deviation

Richard Blake is a writer and broadcaster whose previ-
ous novels have been translated into Italian, Spanish,
Greek, Hungarian, Slovak and Chinese.
He lives in Kent with his wife and daughter.

*I dedicate this book
to my dear wife Andrea
and to my little daughter Philippa*

How I Write Historical Fiction:

Advice from a Practitioner

Richard Blake

(Author of Conspiracies of Rome, *etc, etc)*

London
The Hampden Press
MMXIV

How I Write Historical Fiction:
Advice from a Practitioner, by Richard Blake

First edition published in October 2014

Published by
The Hampden Press
Suite 35
2 Lansdowne Row
London W1J 6HL
England

Paperback ISBN: 978-1502727220

British Library Cataloguing in Publication Data: A catalogue
record for this book is available from the British Library

Printed and bound by CreateSpace

Contents

Introduction

I could have called this short book *How to Write Historical Fiction*. It would arguably have been an accurate title. The book does tell you how to seek your inspiration, and where to do research, and how to find and develop characters, and how to write dialogue and description, and how to integrate the description of background into the main narrative. It even says something about how to find a publisher.

On the other hand, the title I considered and rejected would have created a misleading view of the book. When I pay for a *How to* book, I expect something that takes me, chapter by chapter, though the matter of what I want to learn. *How to Write Historical Fiction* needs to start with a chapter of encouragement—for example, how Philippa Gregory and Steven Saylor have made a pile of cash from their historical novels, and how you can too. It needs to end with a list of the agents who handle historical fiction. Between these points, there must be practical advice on how to write coherent prose, and how to proof a typescript. *How I Write Historical Fiction* is a much better title.

This book is a set of essays, interviews and reviews written between 2011 and 2014. Its most obvious faults are a degree of repetition, and a relentless puffing of my own works. I think these are pardonable faults. When you are answering the same questions, or making the same points, repetition is inevitable. As for the puffing, I wrote mainly to bring people's attention to my novels, and it would have defeated this object not to mention them. In further mitigation, I suggest that the book does contain a great deal of sound advice about the craft of historical fiction. I have spent years dealing with the problems faced by everyone who tries to write an historical novel. How I deal with them has brought me much acclaim. More to the point, it has encouraged Hodder & Stoughton—not an insignificant publisher, I hardly need to say—to commission six novels; and these have been translated so far into Spanish, Italian, Greek, Slovak, Hungarian, Chinese and Indonesian.

Perhaps I am doing many things wrong. At the same time, I must be doing some things right. Such being the case, I offer these reflections as encouragement and advice to anyone who is thinking to enter the most honourable craft that is at once the dearest joy of my life—only excepting my womenfolk—and the main provider of my daily bread.

Richard Blake
Deal, October 2014

Post Scriptum As a further deterrent—or incentive—to the reader, I must say that neither this book nor my novels are for the prudish. Because I do not excel in such things, and because the Internet is filled with the writings of those who do excel, I prefer to avoid close descriptions of the sexual act. What I do not avoid is trying to see things as they are. Nor do I seek to judge these things by any of the standards that have been fashionable during my lifetime. One of the interviews republished here is with *Ulisex*, which is Mexico's leading LGBT magazine. This began as an interview with an Irish gay magazine. It was not published in Ireland. The editor had one look through it, and told me, with rising outrage and hysteria, that his mother had been profoundly shocked by the explanations of the Latin sexual vocabulary and by the translations from the *Epigrams* of Martial. If you are disgusted by the English meanings of words like *fello* and *irrumo* and *paedico* and *futuo* and *cinaedus* and *pathicus* and *tribas*, this is not a book I would encourage you to read. Otherwise, you can find a complete listing of my novels in the Appendix.

A Brief and Rambling Advertisement for the Works of Richard Blake

Oh dear, I suddenly feel just as I always do when I reach the "horrid page" of a job application form. You've given all the easy information—date of birth, qualifications, previous experience, and so forth. You now have a whole sheet of A4 on which you need to explain why the job should be yours. The horridest of horrid pages even contain the words "Continue on a separate sheet if necessary." There's no point shouting "Haven't I said enough already to show whether I can do the bloody job?" No point at all. You've a readership of dead-eyed human resource managers, and they won't even consider having you round for interview until you've revealed your childhood ambition to work in whatever position is being advertised.

It's nearly the same with you lot, my dear readers. It's not enough to know the titles of the books I've written, or where and how to buy them, or to read the reviews, or to be told how they're historically-informed, contain more than a dash of satire and black comedy, and are filled with extreme and graphic violence. No, you want to know all about me as well. The only difference is that, while human resources people—you always excepted, my dear readers, if such is your calling—are a waste of space, you have an absolute right to know about me whatever takes your fancy. The shops are filled with books, and you are at liberty to buy mine or not to buy them. If making a shed load of money from my novels means that I have to open up to you, that's the deal.

So, what to say about me? Try these as the highlights of half a century. Richard Blake: born in Kent; a blissfully happy boy in Kent, then far less happy in South London; crap comprehensive; good university by fluke;

3

next ten years drifting to little obvious effect—estate agency, mini-cabbing, the Law, teaching; Economic and Political Adviser to a Slovak Prime Minister; ringside seat for disintegration of Czechoslovakia; teaching, ghost writing, various modes of troublemaking; married with daughter; living in Deal, in a house where Nelson is said to have slept with Emma Hamilton, and that was certainly once a brothel. Parts of this might make a good novel, though not the sort of novel that I enjoy writing.

Looking at the past few years, I'll simply observe that anyone who becomes a proper writer gives up the time even to look interesting. Most of my life nowadays I spend slumped over a keyboard. When I do sometimes pull myself away from the thing, I'm invariably still thinking about more writing, or about rewriting, or about how to sell more copies. I will always put this aside for my daughter. If my poor wife nags me hard enough, I'll put it aside for her. One day, when I've sold enough books, I hope to become interesting again. For the moment—and any honest writer will confirm this—I am what I write, and I write what I am. If you really want to know me, don't come and look into my blank face. Read my books instead.

Oh, but I need more text to fill up the space I've allotted myself! So, what drew me to writing thrillers set in early seventh century Byzantium? The answer is that I've always wanted to be a writer. In a sense, I've always been one. At school, I much enjoyed the numerous volumes of horror stories published by Pan, and did my best for about a year to imitate their cheerful sick-mindedness. I eventually moved away from these, passing through H.P. Lovecraft and Colin Wilson to M.R. James. But something of their influence remains, I'd never deny. Indeed, the torture scene in *Blood of Alexandria*—the one that made one of its reviewers fell unwell for three days—could easily be excerpted into one of those Pan anthologies.

But, since I'm ultimately an historical novelist, let's

4

talk about my influences here. I read a prose translation of the *Iliad* and *Odyssey* when I was seven, and this began an obsessive interest in the ancient world that has never left me. The first historical novels I read were the *Artor* series by Paul Capon. I read all but one of these when I was eight: I'd have read them all if the last in the series hadn't been stolen from Crofton Park Library. The first adult historical novel I read was *The Egyptian* by Mika Waltari. I read this when I was eleven, and I reread it over and over again until my paperback copy fell apart. By then, I was into Robert Graves—the unexpurgated version of *I Claudius* was most entertaining for one of my still tender years—and into Mary Renault and Alfred Duggan and all the others. You can pick up a lot of history from historical novels. Though a little too didactic by modern standards, *I Claudius* is the best introduction to first century Rome that I know. As for The *Egyptian*, the eighteenth dynasty is more complex, and far more remote from our own assumptions, than Mika Waltari made it. But I think he gets his period more often right than wrong.

But this doesn't say what drew me to seventh century Byzantium. I could say that no one else seems to have done this period. On the other hand, I don't think anyone has done the sixteenth century Ottoman Empire, or fifteenth century China—though I could be wrong here. In my case, during the three years that I systematically played truant from school, I taught myself Latin in the local library so I could read the great classics on which some of my favourite novels were based. I learned quite a lot of Greek under the influence of Mary Renault. The most intensive use I made of this in my teens was to read all the porn that the Loeb editions didn't translate. As an aside, the delicacy of the Loeb editors is a blessing to anyone with a taste for the indecency of the ancients. You take up the parallel text of Martial or the Greek Anthology, and skim the English translation till it switches back into the original or into Italian. This done, you give your attention to the left hand pages.

But I read an abridgement of Gibbon when I was fifteen, and my whole interest in the ancient world settled into its final period of crises and of transition to the world in which we still sort of live. I used him very heavily at university, when I kept myself so far as possible to late Antiquity and the early mediaeval period. I read him in full more than once in my twenties. I last read him in full about ten years ago; and you'll find echoes and whole quotations in *Sword of Damascus*. He may have been mistaken in his estimate of Byzantium. He never realised the enormous pressures on every frontier of the Empire, and only acknowledged in asides the creative and often liberating force of the Christian faith. But his vision of the past remains as compelling now as it was nearly two and a half centuries ago. All discussions of at least the fourth century must begin with Gibbon. His character sketches of Julian and Athanasius, and later of Justinian and Heraclius, have never been bettered.

And for me, it all began to come together in February 2004. The idea for a novel drifted into mind as I was walking through the ruins of Richborough, which used to be the main port of Roman Britain. But I wasn't interested in Richborough as it must have appeared in the great days of the Empire. What interested me was how it must have seemed after the fall of the Empire. What was it like to live amid the physical and spiritual ruins of the Roman Empire? The question came up with greater force when I visited Rome with my wife. Of course, we looked at the Forum and the Coliseum and the ruins of the Imperial Palace, and so forth. But we found ourselves pulled again and again to the remains of Rome dating from or just after the fall of the Western Empire—the fifth century church of St Mary Maggiore, for example, or the many lesser buildings. These were largely intact, and, despite many changes and renovations over the centuries, gave a much more immediate

6

sense of the past than the classical ruins.

At last, in 2005, I set to work on what would become *Conspiracies of Rome*. I wrote this quickly, completing the first draft in six weeks, and it was meant as a diversion for a friend who had recently been diagnosed with terminal bone cancer. He liked the novel, and encouraged me to find a publisher. This was harder said than done, as publishers generally don't look at unsolicited manuscripts, and all the agents I approached either didn't reply or told me to go away. But my friend was persistent, and I eventually published the novel myself. It sold surprisingly well though Amazon; and, at the end of 2006, I was approached by Hodder & Stoughton and asked to revise it for publication as the first in a trilogy. *Conspiracies of Rome* (2008) did well, as did *Terror of Constantinople* (2009) and *Blood of Alexandria* (2010). They did well enough for a second trilogy to be commissioned, and I've now written *Sword of Damascus* (2011) and *Ghosts of Athens* (2012) and *Curse of Babylon* (2013). We shall see what comes after that.

In closing, I'll say that I'm not just the novelist of Byzantium. So far, I've written about a dozen works of non-fiction under another name. In 2011, also under another name, I brought out an alternative history thriller called *The Churchill Memorandum*, which was rather controversial in its reception, though all the reviews have been lavish. And I've recently (October 2014) completed a fantasy novel set in a very bleak England of 2018. One way or the other, my dear readers, I repeat that I intend to make a shed load of money from fiction—certainly enough to let me give up real work. And, if this rambling introduction to the life and thoughts of Richard Blake helps shift those piles of books out of the warehouse, it has not been written in vain.

Why You Should Write a Novel, and How to Do It

I often think of Benjamin Disraeli: "When I want to read a novel," he once said, "I write one." I agree with him. All the pleasure that comes from reading a novel is magnified at least tenfold by the act of writing one. You create a world that may be similar to the one in which we live. Or it may be radically different from any world we know. You populate it with characters who become as real to you as your own loved ones. You have the kind of total, arbitrary control over them and their world that the totalitarian rulers of the twentieth century aimed at but probably never believed possible. Beside all this, the passive act of reading even the greatest works of those far beyond your own ability provides at best a shadowy joy.

I have now written ten novels—twelve, if you include the two abortive though substantial efforts of my younger days. Six of these have been brought out by a most respectable mainstream publisher, with another to follow next year. I have been translated into Spanish, Italian, Hungarian, Slovak, Greek and Complex Chinese and Indonesian. I shall soon begin work on an eleventh—or perhaps a thirteenth—novel. I am contractually obliged to write another one after that. This surely means that, whatever private reservations I may have, I can legitimately say that I am a professional novelist. Such advice as I give, therefore, is based on some experience.

Now, there is only one way to begin. This is to open a blank document in your word processor of choice, and to look at the blinking cursor. If your document is in print layout, and you have set your font to Times New Roman 10pt, you must fill up between 200 and 250 pages. That is somewhere between 85,000 and 160,000 words. Fewer than that, and you may have written a novella. More than that—and many novels do far exceed this count—and you will find yourself with a doorstopper. But 120,000 is a fair average. My own output ranges between these upper and lower limits.

That cursor, flashing black on a perfectly white background is always the most scary part of writing a novel. As said, I suppose I do count as a professional. I still find that white screen utterly paralysing. It is rather like starting a long walk in the mist, and realising that you must, sooner or later, climb over a mountain that you have never seen before. Whether you have written five, or ten, or twenty, or none, let me assure you that the blank opening screen of a new novel is never less than daunting. There are certain games you can play with yourself to blot out the fear of what has to be done. One of my favourites is to open a second document in which I record the number of words written each day. If you have written more than one novel, you can fiddle about with this in moments of despair—to see how your progress this time compares with your last, how this month compares with next month, how much more you need to write before you can lie to yourself that there is a critical mass of words that will carry you of their own momentum to the finish, and so forth. But you never do get away from that flashing black cursor. Oh, and, no matter how much you have written, the same flashing black cursor is there every time you call up the document.

That is how to begin. Where next? Well, beyond the courage of making a start, there are three essentials. The first is that you do need a plot. How you get this I will discuss in a moment. But, unless you are one of those prize-winning sorts, whom everyone praises and nobody reads, you must have something that others will recognise as a story. The second is that you must be able to write English prose. You must be able to spell words, and know their meaning, and be able to put them together in a way that tells your story. You do not need to be a great stylist—or even be that clear about the finer points of grammar. It will do if your readers can understand you, and if they will want to carry on reading you.

The third is that you should know what you are writing about. Most of my novels are thrillers set in the seventh century Byzantine Empire. I write these partly because I like thrillers, and partly because I know a lot about the border period that lies between late Antiquity and the middle ages. It is, I think, an interesting period, and I believe that I have no competition. Certainly, I can put stories against this background and write them up without endless research. I would have trouble writing about—for example—a killer who strikes at football matches, or about a doomed lesbian affair in a Swiss finishing school. I have no interest in these things, and it would take much tedious research to give myself any sort of feel for them. If only at first, you must write about the things you know and that interest you. If you are an estate agent, set your novel in the property market. If you are Jewish, write about Jews. If you have spent your entire adult life as a single mother on a housing estate, write about that. After your first two or three novels, you may be ready to write outside your existing areas of knowledge. Until then, you probably do not understand how to do enough research to avoid being laughed at, and not so much that your novel is years in the writing.

All this being said, how you proceed with a novel is not at all standardised. Some writers, I am told, spend months apparently doing nothing. Only when everything is clear down to the final twist of the plot, do they start writing. They then type with furious energy and have the thing finished in one long and continuous burst. Others begin with a detailed synopsis, and may also fill up pages of character descriptions. Others go through many drafts, and take years to finish. Others write and never change a word thereafter. Others start and see where they will end. Every possible way is equally valid. The only thing that matters is that, eventually, there is a readable manuscript.

I am largely of this final kind. I write at a steady pace, and the plot comes in irregular flashes, a chapter or so ahead of me. In this way, I can finish a novel in about six months. But that is all I can say of my own settled method. Really, I have no settled method. For example, I began my first real novel, *The Column of Phocas*, without knowing what I was about. It was in April 2005. A friend had gone quiet on me. He was not sending out his usual stream of e-mails. He was doing little to answer the e-mails I sent him. He was usually unavailable when I called him. I felt a strange and increasing moral disturbance, and cannot explain why I opened a document in MSWord and began to write a thriller set in Byzantine Rome. All I can say is that I wrote and wrote with total absorption. I had no idea of the plot. I just saw it forming in my head, a chapter ahead of where I was writing. I had the first draft ready in six weeks—just before I managed to bully my friend into taking his terrible bodily aches to a doctor and have it confirmed that he had terminal bone cancer.

I wrote *The Column of Phocas*, then, as a kind of escape from a reality that I must have known in some deeper state of being. I have said that I had no plot. Indeed, I began the last chapter still ignorant of how it would all end. Undoubtedly, since it did result in a readable manuscript, this is one way to write a novel. But it is not something I would recommend. You need to work at a high level of inspiration to produce anything at all. Since I published the novel myself without any revisions—and the typing mistakes do eventually become a catastrophic embarrassment—you can see for yourself how well I succeeded.

My next novel, *Conspiracies of Rome*, was much easier. Indeed, it is semi-complete reworking of *The Column of Phocas*. Now that I had some experience of writing fiction, out came the long historical digressions—cut out altogether, or rewritten into dialogue and action. Out came the eight pages on mediaeval book production—even though I bleated to the publisher about how I needed to slow the plot down before it could be known that Father Maximin had vanished. Out came the reflections on gay sex and on the shift in spoken Greek from a tonic to a stress accent. The result is a great improvement, though I am never sure if, despite its vast changes, *Conspiracies of Rome* counts as a second novel or as a second draft of *The Column of Phocas*.

My next novel, *Terror of Constantinople*, was a new one, however—and it was now that I discovered that blinking cursor. I had no real plot until I was about two thirds through the first draft. All I had at the beginning was a dramatic arrival of my young hero in Constantinople, and then a vision of him near the end, setting out on a journey across the silvery but filthy waters of the Golden Horn. I got this from the film version of *Death in Venice*, and I still think it reads better if you keep in mind the *Adagietto* from Mahler's Fifth Symphony. And that was all I had at the beginning. But, since I knew how it had to end, I was able to keep going until I discovered a plot. At this point, I was able to go back to the start, and—without bothering to complete the first draft—cut and rewrite and insert until everything worked.

For the next one, *Blood of Alexandria*, I tried to industrialise the process by writing out a detailed synopsis. I did manage to keep to this more or less. I did reach the beginning of chapter eight, and then stopped to insert another five chapters that altered the plot fundamentally. I then lost control of the plot just over half way through, and found myself back to making up the plot as I wrote. But I did finish as I had intended. I was rather pleased with the success of the experiment in discipline. But the publisher was of a different opinion, and made me rewrite the last quarter. And that was the last—for the time being, at least—of my starting out with a synopsis.

Sword of Damascus actually began as *Ghosts of Athens*. By the time I had reached chapter three however, I knew that my hero would never see Athens. The previous novels had all begin with a few passages to describe the narrator's life in exile in extreme old age, before he could get down to the main business of writing about the adventures of his youth. But, in this novel, the barbarian siege of the monastery in Jarrow was so real to me that I decided to go on with it, decrepit hero and all. I dropped what I thought a formulaic hunt through mediaeval Athens for something I would announce when I had discovered what it was, and pressed on without any plot at all, but towards a huge climax in the Syrian desert. I ended with what can reasonably be described as a geriatric James Bond novel—or perhaps the novelisation of a Bond film. I wrote it almost as quickly as I had *The Column of Phocas*, and with barely more knowledge of the plot. I think the result is the best thing I have written to date. But I would say that, as it has just been published, and I hope it will be big success.

Because I had written *Sword of Damascus* in a tearing hurry, I had several months free before I had to start on my next Byzantine thriller. I filled this time by writing *The Churchill Memorandum*. This is an alternative history thriller, the starting premise of which is that Hitler died in a car crash in Prague in March 1939. The novel opens in a 1959 where there had been no Second World War, and in which the British Empire still existed in all its glory, and England was still a free country. I began with that premise. As usual, I had no idea what the plot was until I was nearly half way through the first draft. Then, as usual, I put off the ending until I had rewritten the opening chapters. Even then, I only discovered the nature and importance of characters like Harold Macmillan and Michael Foot after I had found myself putting them into the novel.

I think the result has been a success. Certainly, I have

had about half a dozen long reviews for the novel filled with lavish praise. I did think for a while, after its publication in February 2011, that I had made a serious mistake. Without bothering to read it, a whole group of people I thought were my friends—in one case, a friend of thirty years—decided to cast me out of their circle, and have ever since been hinting to anyone who will listen that I am a Nazi. Even after ostentatiously unfriending me on Facebook, one of these has had the nerve to continue posting on my own open Facebook page that I am "swimming in dark waters!" I shall get over being cast out. Other writers I know have had very similar experiences. It seems to go with the territory. If you can avoid it, good luck to you.

And for the avoidance of doubt—*The Churchill Memorandum* is most definitely *not* a nazi novel. If you think the British Empire was one of the high points of world civilisation, and that its collapse was one of the disasters of the twentieth century, you may find it a most enjoyable read. Otherwise, it is a savage black comedy in which I libel every dead person of note in recent British history who has the misfortune to be dead and who is also hated by me!

I will say nothing of *Ghosts of Athens*. I finished this two hours ago, and am writing the present article only because I can think of nothing else to do with it. We shall see how it does when it comes out in 2012. By then, I may feel able to say something about its more than usually chaotic composition.

I did promise to explain something about how to write a novel. You may think I have veered off the subject into autobiography. But there is a point in writing about myself. This is that there is no standard recipe for writing a novel. It depends on the kind of person you are, and also on the mood that you bring to writing it. The important thing is to stop worrying about that flashing black cursor and get on with the business of writing. You need to do that—and you need to keep telling yourself that what you have started will be finished, and will result in a readable manuscript. Between those two points, there is, I will not deny, a hard slog. You will need to cope with days of self-doubt, and even with disgust at that quality of what you have written so far. But there will also be times when the darkness clears a few yards ahead, and a problem of development you never thought would be resolved comes clearly into sight. There will also be that great burst of joy when you have your first draft saved on your hard disk—and backed up on memory stick and in several other places! Do you want to know how I lost three chapters of *Sword of Damascus*, and the latest readable back up dated from the early morning of a very long day? Best not!

Yes, write your novel. It may be good. It may be awful. You may lose friends over it. Your own nearest and dearest may beg you not to share it with the world. But I do promise you that Disraeli gave some very good advice. The greatest and most glorious novel you will ever know is the one you are currently writing.

Fact and Fiction:
The Trouble with Historical Novels

If you describe anything as "the worst thing that can happen," it probably isn't. Whatever you care to imagine, there's usually something worse. But one of the worst things that can happen to an historical novelist is to have someone creep up to you with a smirk on his face, and tell you that some fact in your latest masterpiece is bad history. For me, it's certainly worse than just being told the novel is useless. I've always been sheltered from general criticism behind an impenetrable wall of vanity. I'm a genius. Anyone who says otherwise can only be intellectually or morally defective. Tell me, though, I've got my facts wrong, and I may run screaming from the room.

Of course, when that happens, it's your own fault. The rules of historical fiction are pretty clear. You can write your way into the first century, as secretary to the Emperor Tiberius, and explain that the Emperor always swam alone on Capri—that he was a fine man and ruler, libelled after his death for his Thatcheresque way with the taxpayers' money. You can do that. With a few obvious exceptions, you can blacken or whiten historical characters just as takes your fancy.

What you can't do is write a passage in which someone uncorks a bottle of wine and pours two glasses. You see, everyone who's read Fernand Braudel knows that corked glass bottles only came into use in the seventeenth century, and that glass drinking vessels, though used for thousands of years, only beat metal on the tables of the rich in the same century. You can't get away with that. You will be written off as incompetent. Well, you'll be written off by me as incompetent. You see, I did once get a long way into Taylor Caldwell's *Dear and Glorious Physician*, which is about St Luke the Evangel-

16

ist I put up with everything I didn't like about it until someone in Antioch uncorked a bottle. I threw the book aside at once, and have never ready anything since by its author.

Come to think of it, you'll need to work hard if you want to talk about the taxpayers' money in first century Rome. The central finances drew largely on tribute payments, imposed on each province when it came into the Empire, and were supplemented by confiscation. There were reciprocal obligations between the Emperor and his various kinds of subject. But these weren't based on the same assumptions as govern our relationship with the British State. "My taxes pay your salary" won't get you far with most British State functionaries. The words would probably have got you a very blank look in Ancient Rome.

And so, when writing historical fiction, you need to get your facts right. And this goes beyond looking up on *Wikipedia* when forks or tampons or suntan cream first came into use. You must think yourself into the past age you've chosen, and not make it look as if your characters could have been pulled out of the Underground and sent off into something half way between historical theme park and Big Brother house. You cannot assume that the physical things and habits of thought that you take for granted were the same in the past.

Let me give an example here that only came to my attention last year. I'd been shuffling round National Trust properties since childhood, vaguely noting how short beds were in the past. If asked, I might have explained this by saying that people were shorter in the past. Then, looking through an old book of prints, I realised that persons of quality, before about the early nineteenth century, slept in a sitting position—they didn't need such long beds. Now, I'd always taken my own habit of sleeping in a ball, with the blankets pulled over my head, as a slight deviation from the norm, but never thought of this norm as other than universal.

By the way, this discovery set me into a panic, as there are any number of beds in my own historical novels. Luckily for me, people in the ancient world seem to have slept lying down. But my fingers did tremble as they rattled over the keyboard to call up images of ancient beds.

It worried me for professional reasons, but shouldn't have surprised me. The followers of Karl Marx—and I think here less of Marx himself than of his more unorthodox followers like Karl Polanyi and Moses Finley and Michel Foucault—go too far in claiming that there are no universal norms. They hated bourgeois civilisation, and spent their lives trying to prove that all its norms were part of an order of things that had come recently into existence, and could be hurried back out of existence. In fact, the essentials of human nature don't change. But, if this includes basic motivations, it doesn't include how these are expressed. It can be difficult to work out the difference between motivations and their particular expressions. And there's no doubt that, by our own lights, people in other ages often behaved very oddly.

Oh, look at sex—or, rather, at opinions about sex. Because we are living through a revolution in our own opinions, we are unusually aware of how changeable these things are. I recently went on the radio, to oppose the creeping ban on smoking. One of my arguments was that, if smoking ought to be discouraged because of the burden it allegedly places on health budgets, so should sodomy. Not long ago, I'd have been screamed at for likening smokers to those disgusting homosexuals. Now, Vanessa Feltz accused me of a homophobic hate crime for likening gay people to those filthy, self-harming smokers, and switched off my microphone as soon as she'd finished hyperventilating. How times change!

But, if we are better able than our grandparents to understand how opinions about sex change from one age to another, most people still haven't realised the almost chaotic variation of opinions. I don't think anyone would nowadays write a novel about the ancient world in which most males were exclusively heterosexual, and the occasional homosexual, thrown in for a bit of local colour, was a shrill effeminate. I think here, by the way, of Lance Horner's *Child of the Sun*, which is about the Emperor Heliogabalus and which I much enjoyed as a boy. But, in their sexual manners and laws, the ancients would still be shockingly alien to an ordinary modern audience. Generally speaking, slaves and the lower classes were fair game, regardless of age or gender. His biographer affected shock when Tiberius got semi-weaned babies to suck his penis, because there was some age limit—though this wasn't the sort of limit our sexual purity campaigners would recognise. Equally, when he raped two boys after a sacrifice, and then had their legs broken, he was blamed because they were of good family, and the concluding assault was inhuman regardless of their status. But, whatever he might do to others, a free adult male lost at least his reputation if he was known to take the passive part in oral or anal sex. And the idea of gay marriage seems to have been unknown

If most ordinary readers don't know much about ancient sex, any historical novelist can. There are the works of Kenneth Dover and John Boswell, to name only two of the most readable historians. The problem here is knowing how far to take the readers before they give up in horror. So let me return to the danger of anachronism. Look at language.

Here, I have an advantage over many of my colleagues in the profession. Because my historical novels are set in the seventh century, I don't have to worry about authenticity of words of speech patterns. The convention is that the narrator is writing in a rather classicised Byzantine Greek, and has been translated into a faintly Augustan English. Ideas and words derived from the words of our technological civilisation must always be avoided. Therefore, no one should say that the tem-

19

perature has fallen, or that his anger was fuelled by drink. Nor should he be too specific about times of day, or say that things happened so many seconds apart. No one before the seventeenth century could have used such language. But modern slang and obscenities are appropriate. One of my reviewers picked me up for using the word "shite", which is a moderately recent word. He'd missed the point.

It's the same with stories set in England before about 1500. The language of the characters would have been English—but a fairly remote English, and the pretence can be kept up of a translation. It's harder with stories set here during the seventeenth and eighteenth centuries. You have to be careful here to avoid pastiche. This will fail, as copying the spoken language of an earlier age is much easier to criticise than do well. There's also the risk of confusing readers. I'm not sure if you can say that a plot is discovered, since this word, though much used, had a slightly different meaning before the nineteenth century. And, though you will see it commonly used in *The State Trials*, you will only confuse if you describe someone with dark hair as a black man. Peter Greenaway breaks this rule in his film *The Draughtsman's Contract*. The dialogue is often authentic. I think I even recall a reference, never clarified for the viewers, to the Darien project. But I believe that one of the purposes of this film is to show the past as remote and largely incomprehensible. Mr Greenaway breaks the rules for a specific purpose. He doesn't change them. The rule, I think, is just to avoid using words and expressions that obviously jar as anachronistic—eighteenth century lights can be turned off, never switched off.

For the early twentieth century, the rule is to use your common sense. References to things and persons now obscure, or disused euphemisms—earnest for homosexual, for example, or gay for a prostitute, even perhaps Unionist instead of Conservative—should be avoided. Otherwise, you are lucky that there is hardly anything in

20

the vocabulary or speech patterns of that age that is alien to a modern audience.

I won't boast that I've always got it right in my novels. David Friedman (son of Milton) once got me close to a walking out moment, when he insisted that a glass table I'd put in one of my novels couldn't have been cast before the late middle ages. But I do my best to get things right. At the moment, I'm feeling my way into a novel that involves a plague epidemic. I've therefore learned a lot of new medical history in the past fortnight. Of course, I knew that the germ theory of disease only grew into its modern form after about 1850. I also knew about the late mediaeval quarantines and the biblical rules about seclusion of lepers. What I didn't know was that, until the arrival of syphilis forced the doctors to think again, there was no regular idea of contagion. There seem to have been popular suspicions about the communicability of certain illnesses, and these sometimes forced the authorities to act against the medical advice. But the doctors were mostly committed to the miasma theory of epidemic diseases—invisible clouds of poison that might be evidenced by foul smells.

I still haven't decided what significance plague has in my new novel. Even so, do be assured that it won't just be the look and smell of the sores that I get right.

I could go on and on, but I think I've got across the idea that historical novelists need to pay attention to the historical details, and are judged on how well they do it. On the other hand, you can argue that I'm just a silly pedant, substituting historical research that anyone can do for actual inspiration. I've said that Taylor Caldwell didn't know how the ancients stored and sold their wine. What I haven't said is that her novels remain in print nearly thirty years after her death, and sell in numbers I can only envy—and that her name will probably be remembered when mine has been forgotten.

But that only goes to show how unfair the world can be. After all, haven't I told you—I am a genius!

The Joys of Writing
Byzantine Historical Fiction

As the author of six novels set in seventh century Byzantium, I'm often asked: Why choose that period? There's always been strong interest within the historical fiction community in Classical Greece, and in Rome a century either side of the birth of Christ, and the western Dark Ages. With very few exceptions—Robert Graves' *Count Belisarius*, for example, or Cecelia Holland's *Belt of Gold*—Byzantium in any period of its long history is a neglected area. Why, then, did I choose it?

The short answer is that I wanted to be different. I won't say that there are too many novels set in the other periods mentioned above. There is, even so, a very large number of them. If there is always a market for them, standing out from the crowd requires greater ability than I at first thought I had. And so I began *Conspiracies of Rome* (2008) I ran at once into difficulties I hadn't considered, and that could have been shuffled past had I decided on a thriller about the plot to kill Julius Caesar. Solving these difficulties put me through a second education as a writer, and may even have shown that I do possess certain abilities. Before elaborating on this point, however, let me give a longer answer to my question: Why choose Byzantium?

Looking at our own family history, we tend to pay more attention to our grandparents than our cousins. Whatever they did, we have a duty to think well of our grandparents. We often forget our cousins. So far as they are rivals, we may come to despise or hate them. So it has been with Western Europe and the Byzantine Empire. The Barbarians who crossed the Rhine and North Sea in the fifth century are our parents. They founded a new civilisation from which ours is, in terms of blood and culture, the development. Their history is our history. The Greeks and Romans are our grandparents. In the strict sense, our parents were interlopers who dispossessed them. But the classical and Christian influence has been so pervasive that we even look at our early history through their eyes. The Jews also we shoehorn into the family tree. For all they still may find it embarrassing, they gave us the Christian Faith. We have no choice but to know about them down to the burning of the Temple in 70AD. The Egyptians have little to do with us. But we study them because their arts impose on our senses, and because they have been safely irrelevant for a very long time.

Byzantium is different. Though part of the family tree, it is outside the direct line of succession. In our civilisation, the average educated person studies the Greeks till they were conquered by the Romans, and the Romans till the last Western Emperor was deposed in 476AD. After that, we switch to the Germanic kingdoms, with increasing emphasis on the particular kingdom that evolved into our own nation. The continuing Empire, ruled from Constantinople, has no place in this scheme. Educated people know it existed. It must be taken into account in histories of the Crusades. But the record of so many dynasties is passed over in a blur. Its cultural and theological concerns have no place in our thought. We may thank it for preserving and handing on virtually the whole body of Classical Greek literature that survives. But its history is not our history. It seems, in itself, to tell us nothing about ourselves.

Indeed, where not overlooked, the Byzantines have been actively disliked. Our ancestors feared the Eastern Empire. They resented its contempt for their barbarism and poverty, and its ruthless meddling in their affairs. They hated it for its heretical and semi-heretical views about the Liturgy or the Nature of Christ. They were pleased enough to rip the Empire apart in 1204, and lifted barely a finger to save it from the Turks in 1453. After a spasm of interest in the seventeenth century, the balance of scholarly opinion in the eighteenth and nineteenth centuries was to despise it for its conservatism and superstition, and for its alleged falling away from the Classical ideals—and for its ultimate failure to survive. If scholarly opinion since then has become less negative, this has not had any wider cultural effect. As said, there are few novels set in Constantinople after about the year 600. I am not aware of a single British or American film set there.

I discovered Byzantium when I was fourteen. I was already six years into what has been a lifelong obsession with the ancient world. I had devoured everything I could find and understand about the Greeks between Solon and Alexander the Great, and about the Romans till the murder of Domitian. I was teaching myself Latin, and thinking about Greek. Then, one happy afternoon in my local library, I came across Gibbon's *Decline and Fall of the Roman Empire*. I could, and one day will, write an essay about the literary and philosophical debt I owe him. For the moment, it's enough to say that he led me straight into the so far unexplored history of Late Antiquity and the early Middle Ages. And, though frequently gloomy, what a magnificent history that is. When I studied History at university, I chose every course option that kept me there. Since then, sometimes for years on end, I've buried myself in the unfolding story of the Byzantine Empire. Hardly surprising that, when I turned to historical fiction, my first and only choice should be Byzantium.

Of course, I revere Classical Antiquity. But, once your eyes adjust, and you look below the glittering surface, you see that it wasn't a time any reasonable person would choose to be alive. The Greeks were a collection of ethnocentric tribes who fought and killed each other till they nearly died out. The Roman Empire was held together by a vampire bureaucracy directed more often than in any European state since then by idiots or lunatics. Life was jolly enough for the privileged two or three per cent. But everything they had was got from the enslavement or fiscal exploitation of everyone else.

Now, while the Roman State grew steadily worse until the collapse of its Western half, the Eastern half that remained went into reverse. The more Byzantine the Eastern Roman Empire became, the less awful it was for ordinary people. This is why it lasted another thousand years. The consensus of educated opinion used to be that it survived by accident. Even without looking at the evidence, this doesn't seem likely. In fact, during the seventh century, the Empire faced three challenges. First, there was the combined assault of the Persians from the east and the Avars and Slavs from the north. Though the Balkans and much of the East were temporarily lost, the Persians were annihilated. Then a few years after the victory celebrations in Jerusalem, Islam burst into the world. Syria and Egypt were overrun at once. North Africa followed. But the Home Provinces—these being roughly the territory of modern Turkey—held firm. The Arabs could sometimes invade, and occasionally devastate. They couldn't conquer.

One of the few certain lessons that History teaches is that, when it goes on the warpath, you don't face down Islam by accident. More often than not, you don't face it down at all. In the 630s, the Arabs took what remained of the Persian Empire in a single campaign. Despite immensely long chains of supply and command, they took Spain within a dozen years. Yet, repeatedly and with their entire force, they beat against the Home Provinces of the Byzantine Empire. Each time, they were thrown back with catastrophic losses. The Byzantines never lost overall control of the sea. Eventually, they hit back, retaking large parts of Syria. More than once, the Caliphs were forced to pay tribute. You don't manage this by accident.

The Byzantine historians themselves are disappointingly vague about the seventh and eight centuries. Our only evidence for what happened comes from the description of established facts in the tenth century. As early as the seventh century, though, the Byzantine State pulled off the miracle of reforming itself internally while fighting a war of survival on every frontier. Large parts of the bureaucracy were scrapped. Taxes were cut. The silver coinage was stabilised. Above all, the great senatorial estates of the Later Roman Empire were broken up. Land was given to the peasants in return for military service. In the West, the Goths and Franks and Lombards had moved among populations of disarmed tax-slaves. Not surprisingly, no one raised a hand against them. Time and again, the Arabs smashed against a wall of armed freeholders. A few generations after losing Syria and Egypt, the Byzantine Empire was the richest and most powerful state in the known world.

This is an inspiring story—as inspiring as the resistance put up by the Greek city states a thousand years before to Darius and Xerxes. Why write yet another series of novels about the Persian or Punic wars, when a lifetime of research had given me all this as my background? You can ask again: Why Byzantium? My answer is: What else but Byzantium?

And so I've written six novels set in the seventh century, mostly within the great cities of the Byzantine Empire. The background in each is the wavering but increasingly successful struggle to break free of the Roman heritage. *Conspiracies of Rome* (2008) is a kind of prelude. It explains how Aelric, the hero of the entire series—young and beautiful and clever, at least two of which things I'm not—is kicked out of Anglo-Saxon England, and comes to Rome to try his luck. At once, he trips head first into the snake pit of Imperial politics, and doesn't climb out again until the body count runs into dozens. In *Terror of Constantinople* (2009), he's tricked into a mission to Constantinople, where we see the old order of things falling apart in a reign of terror. In *Blood of Alexandria* (2010), he's come up in the world, and is in Egypt as the Emperor's legate, sent there to impose a

26

plan of land reform—which is, you can be sure, entirely his idea. Faced with a useless Viceroy, an obstructive landed interest, and an intrigue featuring the first chamber pot of Jesus Christ and the mummy of Alexander the Great, everything goes tits up, and there's a climax in an underground complex near to the Great Pyramid.

The next two novels in the series are an apparent digression from the overall scheme. In *Sword of Damascus* (2011), a very aged Aelric is kidnapped from his place of refuge and retirement in the North of England and carted off to the heart of the Islamic Caliphate. *Ghosts of Athens* (2012) returns us to the immediate aftermath of Aelric's less than triumphant efforts in Egypt. I did intend this to be a tightly-constructed thriller set in a horribly broken down Athens. It turned instead into a gothic horror novel—quite a good one, I think; a surprise for the reader, even so.

In *Curse of Babylon* (2013), I return to Imperial high politics, complete with a Persian a Great King who is described by one of the reviewers as "possibly the most sadistic fictional bad guy I've ever encountered." Because I don't think I shall write any more in the series, I made *Curse of Babylon* the most expansive and spectacular of the whole set. It has kidnaps and daring escapes, blood and sex everywhere, acrobatic fights that owe much to Hollywood at its best, and a gigantic battle at the climax.

I suppose there is room for another three or even six. But I'll not be thinking about that this year, or next year, or perhaps the year after that. My latest novel, *The Break* (2014)—written under another name—is postapocalyptic science fiction. This will be followed by a horror novel set in York.

I haven't bothered with detailed outlines of the six Byzantine novels. What I will say, however, is that I've worked very hard not to make any of them into a factual narrative enlivened by a bit of kissing and a few sword fights. I greatly admired Jean Plaidy as a boy, and she taught me as much as I still know about France during the Wars of Religion. But I don't regard her as a model for writing historical fiction. So far as we can know or reconstruct them, the facts must always be respected. Indeed, I would say that anyone who wants a reliable introduction to the world of seventh century Byzantium could do worse than start with my novels. Even so, these are novels, and they must stand or fall as entertainment. The plots have to keep the reader guessing and turning the pages. The characters have to live and breathe. Their language and actions need to be credible.

Rather than argue that this is what I've achieved, let me quote from one of the reviews. According to *The Morning Star*, I give readers "a near-perfect blend of historical detail and atmosphere with the plot of a conspiracy thriller, vivid characters, high philosophy and vulgar comedy." Another reviewer has called me "the Ken Russell of historical fiction." I don't think this was meant to be a compliment, but I'll take it as one.

I come now to the difficulty I mentioned in my second paragraph. If you want to write a novel about the plot to kill Caesar, you can leave my readers to supply much of the background. From Shakespeare to Rex Warner and beyond, the reading and the viewing public know roughly what is going on. Everyone likely to buy such a novel knows that Rome had expanded from a city state to an empire, and that its constitution had broken down in the process. Everyone knows that Caesar was ruling as a military dictator, and that this was resented by much of the senatorial aristocracy. Everyone knows who Cicero was, and Mark Antony, and Cleopatra. If you want to write about this, you can largely get on with the plot. You may need to go into a few details about the theoretical legality of Caesar's power, or the oddities of the Roman electoral system. But much of the job has already been done for you.

You can't do this with seventh century Byzantium. The reading public can't be expected to know much at all. You have a continuing Roman Empire after Rome itself has fallen. Paganism is out. Instead, you have a legally established Christian Faith, with ranting clerics whose differing views of the Nature of Christ are turning the Empire into a patchwork of mutually-hostile classes and nationalities. You have a crumbling tax base and an omnipresent threat on the borders with Persia. Later, you have militant Islam. Because readers can't be expected to know this, you have to tell them.

In *Claudius the God*, Robert Graves explains the obscure facts of Roman policy in the East with what amounts to a long essay. It's a good essay. But you can't do this nowadays. Fashions have changed. Readers are less patient. They want a story to keep moving. You need to integrate your background into the action and dialogue.

I didn't get this entirely right in *Conspiracies of Rome*. There's an authorial explanation at the start of the second section of the novel. This works, but displeased my editor at Hodder & Stoughton. So I worked like a slave on *Terror of Constantinople* and the other four novels to give my editor exactly what she wanted. In Terror, I allowed myself one explanation of background, but put this into a dialogue between Aelric and a drunken slave who needs to be told about the civil war between Phocas and Heraclius to make sense of a failed murder attempt. In *Sword of Damascus*, old Aelric is allowed to turn garrulous once or twice when the fourteen year-old English boy he has with him asks questions about the world they've entered. On the whole, though, I'm proud of how I eventually got past what seemed an insuperable barrier to writing popular historical fiction set in a fairly unknown period.

It's easier to show than to describe. But how you do it is a matter of casual asides and revealed assumptions. You pick up what is happening in much the same way as you might from an overheard conversation. To give one example from an alternative history novel I wrote a few

29

years ago, something is described as being "about the same size as a self-charging television battery." You get the size of the object described from the context. The purpose of the comparison is to tell the reader something more about the technology available. Continue with this throughout the whole course of a novel, and you explain your background without slowing the pace.

I turn to the language in these novels. I don't face the same problems as I might with a novel set in England or America before about 1900. Because the pretence here is that Aelric is writing his memoirs in Greek, I can give a translation into reasonably idiomatic English—reasonably idiomatic, that is, because a faint Augustanism creates a sense of distance. No one has complained about the faint echoes of Gibbon or Congreve. But there have been complaints about the swearing. One of the American reviewers even says that the books should be R-rated for all the rude words in them. My answer is that this is how people have always spoken. Though heroic and often noble, Aelric is a cynical opportunist. He is always eager to think the worst of people, and to write about them in matching terms.

The reviewer also complained about the extreme and graphic violence. If I never trouble the reader with graphic descriptions of the sexual act—like most other people, I'm useless at writing porn, and there's tons of it nowadays on the Internet to suit every taste—my novels are drenched in violence. Another American reviewer said that the torture chamber passages in *Blood of Alexandria* made him feel unwell for several days. My answer again is that this is how it was, and still is. No government has ever lasted without at least the threat of the executioner and the torture chamber. I see no point in hiding the disgusting means by which power is generally got and maintained.

This has turned out to be a somewhat longer advertisement for my novels than I intended, or was asked, to write. So I'll conclude by saying that, if you like the sound of them, please consider buying my novels. I think they're rather good. More to the point, so do the reviewers. You should probably begin at the beginning with Conspiracies of Rome, though Sword of Damascus is my own favourite.

All else aside, they make ideal presents for those hard-to-please loved ones.

Interview with Richard Blake for *Circa*: *A Journal of Historical Fiction*, July 2014

Richard Blake has so far written these historical novels, all published in London by Hodder & Stoughton, and all set in the Byzantine Empire of the seventh century:

Conspiracies of Rome by Richard Blake (2008)
The Terror of Constantinople by Richard Blake (2009)
The Blood of Alexandria by Richard Blake (2010)
The Sword of Damascus by Richard Blake (2011)
The Ghosts of Athens by Richard Blake (2012)
The Curse of Babylon by Richard Blake (2013)
What was your original inspiration for Aelric?

Based on the similarity in their names, is there any special connection readers are meant to draw between Aelric and the historical figure of Alaric, the Visigoth who sacked Rome in the fifth century?

I think the first idea came to me in the February of 2005, when my wife took me for a long weekend break in Rome. This was my first visit to the City, and my first at that time of year to anywhere in the Mediterranean World. In both senses, the visit opened my eyes. It was cold—much colder than England. Though I "knew" otherwise from the sources, I'd had a fixed notion of the ancient world as a place of omnipresent sun and warmth. Stumbling round the Forum in thick overcoat and gloves brought everything closer to my own experience, and set me thinking about what the Romans wore in winter, and how often most of them really bathed, and what the air must have been like in a place where a quarter of a million houses were heated with charcoal.

More important perhaps was the state of what remained from the past. The Forum had a melancholy grandeur. The Colisseum was vast even by the standards of London. The Basilica of Constantine must have been bigger than St Paul's. But, excepting the Pantheon, and those parts of buildings made into churches, everything was in ruins—noble ruins, I'll grant, but ruins even so. Everywhere I looked, there was the sense of something that was over and done with.

But I found many churches than I'd expected going back to the sixth or fifth or even fourth centuries. Though always added to, or changed in other ways, these carried me back—far more effectively than the broken stones of the Temple of Jupiter—to the days of Antiquity. And they were often astonishingly lovely in their own right. Take, for example, the Church of St Mary Maggiore. Built in the early fifth century, and more or less unchanged in its interior, this was a place where the senatorial aristocracy had come to worship, and had been used in unbroken sequence ever since for worship.

If surprised, though, I wasn't disappointed. Ever since my first reading of Gibbon as a boy, my interest had been as much in the end of Antiquity as in its great days. At university, I'd focussed so far as possible on the early Middle Ages. Since then, if in a desultory manner, I'd been going through the history and literature of the Byzantine Empire. Finding so many connections to it in Rome was an unexpected bonus to the visit. By the second day, my wife and I had given up on the usual monuments. Instead, with a new and bigger guide book, we explored Rome from the early Middle Ages to the Renaissance. Every time we came out from somewhere grand and wonderful, we asked each other what it must have been like to visit or live in a Rome when these buildings were new, but still surrounded by the intact if decaying remains of the Imperial City. That, I think, was the first inspiration for my Byzantine novels.

A few months later, my mother lent me half a dozen assorted thrillers set in Ancient Rome. I won't say who wrote these, though none was by Steven Saylor—the Grand Master of the *genre*. A couple were excellent. I thought the rest were dire. "Can you do any better?" she asked when I'd finished sneering at the blunders of fact and atmosphere and plotting and characterisation. "Bet you I can," I said straight back. "Go on, then," she laughed. "Bring it round when you've done it."

A few days later, I opened a new file in MS Word, and sat staring at the cursor. I was going to write a novel. I'd already written two novels in my twenties. But these had been about as dire as the ones I'd denounced to my mother, and were trapped on 5.25" floppies formatted for an obsolete computer. I was going to write an historical thriller. It would be set right at the end of Antiquity, and would take place in Rome. Where to start?

My answer was to make an Englishman the hero and narrator. You can give the lead in historical fiction to a complete foreigner. All you need is someone reasonably attractive to the readers. But I wasn't sure how much ability I had. Besides, one of my favourite historical novels is Cecelia Holland's *City of God*, which has an Englishman as the lead character. When I was a boy, I enjoyed Paul Capon's *Artor* series, which, even in the volume set in Minoan Crete, has a leading character with some connection to this island. Also, when at university, I read a very good novel, written for children, about the Fall of Constantinople to the Turks in 1453. The lead character in this was a boy from Bristol. So it was be a thriller set c600 in Rome, and the lead character would be an Anglo-Saxon. What next?

My answer here was to Google a list of Anglo-Saxon names. I didn't fancy names like Edmund, Edward, Alfred, and so forth. Nor did I fancy names that no one would be able to pronounce. At last, my eyes stopped on Aelric. Almost but not quite familiar, and not impossible to pronounce. So I had my character. Now, what to do with him?

Here, I feel obliged to discuss how I write. Some

novelists make up a detailed plan in advance, listing all the characters, and summarising each part of the story, or even each chapter. I can't do this. After ten novels, I no longer feel ashamed to say that whatever plan I make will become obsolete within a few pages. Sometimes, I'll start with an image of where I want to end. In *Terror of Constantinople* (2009), I started with the idea of Aelric, beautiful in white, standing on a boat as it moves across the shining but filthy waters of the Golden Horn. In *Sword of Damascus* (2011), I started with a vague idea of a climax in the Syrian desert. But that's the best I can ever do. For the rest, I make the story up a chapter at a time. If it comes quickly, as it normally does, I can write a novel in four months. If it dribbles out like an old man's urine—as happened with *Curse of Babylon* (2013)—I'll take nine months.

The critics often say that my plots are unpredictable, but still manage to follow a logical course. The reason for this is that I generally write without knowing what will happen next, but keep going back to change what I've already written. Give me a pen or a typewriter, and I'd never get anything written. Let me die before finishing a novel, and anyone brought in to finish it for me would find a chaotic mass of words. The nice thing about living at the start of the computer age is that everything can be sorted as it approaches the end. The readers see only the finished product, and this is a coherent structure that looks as if it was all written to plan. When I read one of my novels, what I see is paragraphs and block of paragraphs, or just single sentences, that were written for one purpose and used for another. For me, It's like looking at a set of geological strata that have been pressed and buckled by endless movements of the earth.

Back, however, to the first novel. I began with the idea that Aelric would be telling his story in extreme old age, and that he'd be writing about himself in his early or middle teens. I wanted someone of astonishing beauty, who'd be ruthless and uninhibited in his tastes, and who could be lusted over by monsters of both sexes. But early and middle teens didn't work. I needed him also to be very strong and reasonably well-educated. Because I still needed youth and beauty, I spent the whole novel dithering over his age. I finally settled on nineteen. Except in *Sword of Damascus*, where he's pushing a hundred, the whole series follows Aelric to the age of twenty five.

Once I'd realised the plot would reveal itself, I wrote the first novel six weeks. I wrote so quickly because I fell in love with the project, and worked on it on railway trains and even replacement busses. It took over my life, and I almost lived in seventh century Rome. Then there is the sad story of a friend's terminal illness. He'd been complaining for several months about aches and pains legs and lower back. Everyone put this down to the fact that he was getting old—he was 55—and his insistence on jogging and roller skating as if he were still in his twenties. But I felt an increasing sense of dread every time we met or spoke on the telephone. I couldn't see it at the time. Looking afterwards at the photographs, however, it was plain that he had the mark of death on his face. I completed my draft two days before he told me that he might have bone cancer. My first Byzantine novel, then, was a kind of moral anaesthesia.

But you ask about Aelric's double name. Here is the passage in *Conspiracies of Rome* where it begins:

> "Martin handles all my correspondence with the East" the Dispensator explained. "Though growing up in Constantinople, he is originally from an island to the west of Britain. I can assure you, however, he is neither a Celtic heretic nor a Greek semi-schismatic. He is a true son of the Church. He has my trust in all things. He has drawn an entry permit for the young man to our own library."

> Martin handed over a sheet of parchment covered in the smooth, clear hand of the Roman Chancery.

The Dispensator continued:

"He has also drawn an introduction to Anicius, an elderly nobleman of eccentric views who still has a library in his house. You'll not find much there of spiritual sustenance. But one must read the pagan classics for their style."

Martin handed over another sheet drawn in similar form.

The Dispensator paused, looking at Maximin. Martin remained where he was and coughed gently.

"Oh, yes. The young man"—he squinted at my name on the report—"Alaric, is it not? Is that a Gothic name?"

I didn't correct the error. So began my life as Alaric rather than as Aelric. (Chapter 8)

Don't ask me why I did this. It just came out as I wrote. Nor ask why, having done it, I left it in. Had I known this was the start of six novels, I'd have cut it out. On the other hand, Aelric is a name most Greeks and Romans would have had trouble pronouncing, and they'd have changed it to something else. Also, it comes in handy to mark when Aelric and Martin are speaking as friends in a language no one else can understand.

What, if any, are the challenges for you as a fiction writer in depicting historical figures as opposed to your own invented characters? How do you overcome these challenges?

I don't know how I'd write a novel about Hitler or Elizabeth I. With them, you're stuck with known personalities. Showing them as other than wax dummies can be difficult. In my *Churchill Memorandum* (2011), written under another name, I bring in much of the mid-twentieth century British political establishment. But this is an alternative history satire, set in a world where the Second World War hadn't happened. I can do as I please with my characters. In the real world of 1959, Michael Foot wasn't a strangler who got rid of the evidence in an acid bath, and Harold Macmillan wasn't a traitor and camp homosexual. In my alternative 1959, I could turn everyone who actually existed into a grossly defamatory caricature.

In my Byzantine novels, there are only half a dozen characters who really existed. The main ones are the Emperors Phocas and Heraclius, the General Priscus, and the King of Persia. Except they were rather unpleasant, we know very little about any of them. There was no Herodotus or Suetonius or Tacitus to tell us how they behaved or what they said. This means I can treat them as I please. Phocas is a kind of Stalin. Heraclius may be a clever politician or a dithering fool. Chosroes is a raving maniac. If Priscus were brought back to life, he might be flattered by what I've done with him. But the main answer to this question is that your problem doesn't arrive. The real characters might as well be fictional for all I need to pay attention to my sources.

When it comes to researching the period, what are your main sources? Are there any specific challenges in researching Late Antiquity?

The main challenge for my period is a lack of sources. Our main sources for the sixth century are Procopius and Agathius, who were first rate historians in the Classical tradition. For the early seventh century, our main source is Theophanes, an indifferent chronicler from a few hundred years later, George of Pisidia, an indifferent court poet, and a mass of fragments and ecclesiastical writings. Whether in translation or the original, you can master all the Greek and Latin primary sources in a couple of days. Throw in everything in Armenian, Arabic and Syriac, and you may need another week. The secondary sources are more voluminous, and often useful. But you don't have the shelf miles of books and newspapers and government records you need to go through to write a convincing novel about life and death in the trenches or the Blitz or the American Civil War.

What this means is that I have to use the more detailed records of adjoining periods to extrapolate. I need to write according to the spirit of what emerges from the sources. This gives me great freedom. At the same time, those facts that we do have, or can reasonably guess, must be given full respect. I can justly say that I know my stuff. I have read everything available in English, Latin, Greek and French on the period. Even hostile critics have never accused me of ignorance or deliberate inaccuracy. Indeed, I can promise that, if you are an undergraduate who needs a good introduction to the world of the seventh century, my Byzantine novels are a good place to start.

Do you do the bulk of your research before you begin writing the story or do you research as you go along?

In my case, it's the latter. In *Blood of Alexandria*, for example, I read hundreds of pages on the government of Egypt and the various shades of the Monophysite heresy before I started work. But I then read hundreds more as I worked.

Indeed, every now and again, a stray fact picked up while looking for others has found its way into the structure. In *Ghosts of Athens*, I found that I needed to know whether the Long Walls existed into the early Middle Ages. While going through a dozen journal articles, I noticed that, though part of the Eastern Empire and Greek-speaking, the See of Corinth answered to the Pope rather than the Patriarch of Constantinople. This gave me the idea of using Athens as the venue for a closed council of the Eastern and Western Churches.

Of course, the volume of research diminished as the series continued. In *Conspiracies of Rome*, you won't believe the number of maps and chronologies I had open on my computer as I wrote. By the time I reached *Curse of Babylon* (2013), I had nearly all the factual background in my head. All I distinctly remember looking up was what people believed about astrology, and whether women could serve in the bureaucracy—oh, and reams of stuff about the reform of the silver coinage in 615.

It is a truism that historical fiction has more to say about the contemporary world than about the period in which the work is set. Nevertheless, do you see any meaningful parallels between Aelric's world and the present?

I could write at length on this question, but won't. I am monstrously opinionated about politics and economics, among much else. Everything I write has some connection with my libertarian-High Tory view of the world. I try to keep this under control in the novels. The trouble about political novels of any ideology is that they too often veer across the border between entertainment and propaganda. But I am an ideologue, and this shows through in my fiction. I believe that government is, in itself, a bad thing, and that most other bad things are made worse by government. The world would be a better place without all the vast structures of control that now constrain our lives. I hope you will see this belief in my fiction. I also hope it doesn't hit you over the head.

What do you think is the biggest misconception among readers about Byzantium?

The biggest misconception appears to be that the Byzantine Empire was a sterile, gloomy place, devoid of interest to anyone but Orthodox Christians or historians who are the scholarly equivalent of train spotters. There is enough truth in this charge for it to have stuck in the popular imagination for the past few centuries. With exceptions like Cecelia Holland's *Belt of Gold*, there is no Byzantine sub-genre in historical fiction. I can think of no British or American films set in Constantinople after about the year 600—and few before then.

Undoubtedly, the Byzantines made little effort to be original in their literature. But they had virtually the whole body of Classical Greek literature in their libraries and in their heads. For them, this was both a wonderful possession and a fetter on the imagination. It was in their language, and not in their language. Any educated Byzantine could understand it. But the language had moved

40

on—changes of pronunciation and dynamics and vocabulary. The classics were the accepted model for composition. But to write like the ancients was furiously hard. Imagine a world in which we spoke Standard English, but felt compelled, for everything above a short e-mail, to write in the language of Shakespeare and the Authorised Version of the Bible. Some of us might manage a good pastiche. Most of us would simply memorise the whole of the Bible, and, overlooking its actual content, write by adapting and rearranging remembered clauses. It wouldn't encourage an original literature. Because Latin soon became a completely foreign language in the West—and because we in England were so barbarous, we had to write in our own language—Western Mediaeval literature is often a fine thing. The Byzantine Greeks never had a dark age in our sense. Their historians in the fifteenth century wrote up the fall of Constantinople to the Turks in the same language as Thucydides. Poor Greeks.

But you really need to be blind not to see beauty in their architecture and their iconography. Though little has survived, they were even capable of an original reworking of classical realism in their arts.

Above all, Byzantine history is a record of survival and even prosperity in the face of terrible odds. Between about 540 and 720, the Byzantines were hit by wave after wave of catastrophe. First, there was the Great Plague of the 540s, that killed around a third of the population. Then, in the first decades of the seventh century, they were attacked on every frontier by the Persians and the Barbarians. They saw off these challenges, but had no time to recover before the first eruption of Islam from the deserts. In almost a single bite, the Arabs swallowed up the remains of the Persian Empire. They conquered vast areas of the East, and, within less than a century, pushing into Southern France. But, if they took Syria and Egypt and North Africa, they never conquered the core territories of the Byzantine Empire.

41

The reason for this is that the Byzantine State was ruled by creative pragmatists. The Roman Empire was a ghastly place for most of the people who lived in it. The Emperors at the top were often vicious incompetents. They ruled through an immense and parasitic bureaucracy. They were supreme governors of an army too large to be controlled. They protected a landed aristocracy that was a repository of culture, but that was ruthless in its exaction of rent. Most ordinary people were disarmed tax-slaves, where not chattel slaves or serfs.

During the seventh century, the Byzantines scrapped almost the entirety of the Roman heritage. Much of the bureaucracy was shut down. Taxes were cut. The silver coinage was stabilised. Above all, the landed estates were broken up and given to those who worked on them, in return for service in local militias. Though never abolished, chattel slavery became far less pervasive. The civil law was simplified, and the criminal law humanised—after the seventh century, the death penalty was rarely used.

The Byzantine Empire survived because of a revolutionary transformation in which ordinary people became armed stakeholders. The inhabitants of Roman Gaul and Italy and Spain barely looked up from their ploughs as the Barbarians swirled round them. The citizens of Byzantium fought like tigers in defence of their country. Now, this was a transformation pushed through in a century and a half of recurrent crises during which Constantinople itself was repeatedly under siege. Alone among the ancient empires in its path, Byzantium faced down the Arabs, and kept Islam at bay for nearly five centuries.

Don't tell me this isn't an inspiring story. I could have written yet another series of novels around the Persian War or the murder of Julius Caesar. But, if you can take the trouble to master your sources—and never let them master you—I really can't think of a finer background than the early flowering of the one of the most remarkable, and effectively democratic, civilisations that ever existed.

What other writers inspire you, in terms of genre, craft or both?

Where historical fiction is concerned, I grew up on Mika Waltari and Mary Renault and Robert Graves. More recently, there was Gore Vidal and Patrick O'Brien and Steven Saylor. But I can't say how many historical novels I've devoured. When I was in my teens, I could read three or four a week. For other novelists, I admire Wilkie Collins and Conan Doyle and H. Rider Haggard. Oh, and there's Rafael Sabatini and the Baroness Orczy. But there really are so many, living and dead.

But what I like in a novelist or whatever kind is a good story and a sense of realism—even when, as with Rider Haggard, the story is pure fantasy. This is my chief objection to literary fiction. I simply can't enjoy D.H. Lawrence and Virginia Woolf and James Joyce and all the others. Their stories are depressing and unrealistic. Their style is obtrusive and self-referential. For all her later faults, I think Barbara Cartland was a better writer than Iris Murdoch.

Readers and aspiring writers are always interested: what was your path to publication?

I've said I wrote two novels in my younger days. Full of hope, I sent these off to dozens of publishers and agents. Of course, I got nowhere. Most didn't reply. Most who did got my hope up by asking for the manuscript only so they could drop it in the nearest bin and keep the return postage.

I could have tried self-publication, but this was too expensive. Even if I avoided the vanity press sharks, and went to a reputable printer, it was expensive. It involved various kinds of typesetting and proofing, and printing and binding. Once these fixed costs were taken into account, you had to order several thousand copies to get your unit costs close to a viable retail price. And how was I to sell these? Newspapers and magazines didn't review self-published books. The main booksellers didn't stock them. Getting into the bibliographical databases was beyond me. Without an ISBN, a book couldn't be ordered. I'd have had a hundred heavy boxes to store, and a marketing strategy that was confined to lineage advertisements and taking a dozen copies at a time to conferences and other meetings where I might find readers.

Since no one would publish me, I gave up on fiction, and turned to political pamphleteering. Then, in the 1990s, I took to the Internet, and published about a million words on my own websites. This was all rather controversial, but it got me a name and an audience, and it was free. I didn't realise at the time that I was getting ready for my next entry to the fiction market.

When I wrote the first version of *Conspiracies of Rome*, I took it for granted that no one else would publish it, so decided to bring it out myself. By now, the information technology revolution had brought down unit costs even in small runs. I had already published out several books of my Internet writings, and was pretty good at formatting in MS Word, and in designing covers in MS Publisher. So I called my novel *The Column of Phocas* and sent it off to a printer in the West of England.

Oh, the arrogance of doing that! I've said I wrote the novel in about six weeks. I sent it off to the printer after the briefest and most negligent proofing. It came back with missed full stops and dropped speech marks. There were fragments of sentences that I revised as I wrote and left undeleted. I had an eccentric taste in punctuation. In particular, I didn't see the point in putting a comma before a closing speech mark in an unfinished sentence. I was also rather hazy about whether full stops should be inside or outside closing speech marks. Note: they can be either—but you must choose one standard, and stick to it.

Worse, its pace is variable. Unless you're a genius,

this is something learned by practice. The story in a modern novel must be told almost wholly by way of dialogue and action. Speaking about novels in general, every sentence must contribute to the plot. Digressions that don't somehow contribute must be ruthlessly cut out. I didn't know this at the time. I told myself I was writing fiction set in a virtually unknown period, and that the occasional digression was needed if readers were to understand the plot. I do this better now. When I started, I barely understood the difficulties.

And there is too much swearing. Yes, I know that characters in an historical novel must speak, *mutatis mutandis,* as if they were alive now—"'Gadzooks,' quoth he, 'thou hast thyself well-acquitted this day,'" is unacceptable. But did I need quite so much effing and blinding? I think the answer is no. Since then, I've become more varied in my dialogue. In my latest novel. *The Break*, there is no swearing at all.

Nevertheless, the book was a hit. I sold a thousand copies to my mailing list, and got some good reviews. One day, feeling more than usually pleased with myself, I dashed off a letter and sent it to a few dozen publishers. I explained that the novel was doing well, and it might do better still with a real publisher behind it—and that we might all make a tidy profit from this. Within a week, I had three replies and two offers. I signed with Hodder & Stoughton, and *Conspiracies of Rome* is a substantial rewrite of *The Column of Phocas*—a rewrite in which I was nagged into correcting all the faults I now find in it.

I've now done six novels with Hodder. These have all had nice reviews, and have been translated so far into Spanish, Italian, Greek, Slovak, Hungarian, Indonesian and Chinese. Other languages will follow. I used to feel embarrassed about calling myself a writer. But If this doesn't make me one, I don't know what else will.

I got my break into the mainstream by lucky accident. My letters arrived at just the right time. I don't know if the strategy I adopted will work for someone else—though I'll not discourage anyone from trying it. I got in before the big financial crash, and before the publishing market began to turn upside down in response to the rise of e-books. Times have fundamentally changed even in the past few years.

But times have changed fundamentally in the interests of authors. I won't knock Hodder & Stoughton. My editors there have taught me many things I might not otherwise have realised I needed to learn. The company has exposed me to a much wider audience, at home and abroad, than I'd ever have been able to reach by my own efforts. All the same, we live in an age of disintermediation. Authors are no longer obliged to beat themselves against the door of the corporate publishing industry like flies against a window pane. We can do it ourselves. Between two of my Hodder novels, I wrote my alternative history satire, *The Churchill Memorandum*. I didn't even think to offer it to a publisher. It went straight to Kindle, and has been doing well ever since. My latest novel, *The Break* is a post-apocalyptic thriller which is also a brutal satire on our leftist managerial state. This also I brought out myself. It came out in July 2014, and has already been nominated for the 2015 Prometheus Award.

So, good luck if you can get a juicy publishing contract. But you probably won't, and the future is to do it yourself.

Are there other historical periods that you want to write about someday?

I've been considering a thriller set in 1690s London—another underused period full of excitement and colour. The protagonist will be a woman playwright caught up in a mystery about a sealed package of documents. Depending on other commitments, I may start work on this next year.

What question do you wish I had asked but didn't? How would you answer it?

Bearing in mind the length of the answers I've given so far, it may be for the best if I pass on this question.

Interview with *Ulisex* **Magazine,**
October 2014

You're a historical novelist, which confuses some
people when they come across it first! What does it
mean, and how do you blend fact and fiction together
through it?

As a specific genre, the historical novel is only about
two centuries old. Historical fiction in the wider sense,
though, is at least as old as the written word. *The Epic of
Gilgamesh*, the Homeric poems, the narrative books of
the Old Testament, *Beowulf*—the earliest literature of
every people is historical fiction. The past is interesting.
It's glamorous and exciting. Perspective allows us to
forget that the past, like the present, was mostly long
patches of boredom or anxiety, mixed in with occasional
moments of catastrophe or bliss. Above all, it's about us.

Have you ever stared at old family pictures, and had
the feeling that you were looking into a mirror? I have a
photograph of a great uncle, who was an old man before
I was born. I never knew him well. But in that picture,
taken when he was about fifteen, he has my ears and
eyes, and he's hugging himself and looking just as com-
placent as I often do. I have a picture of one of my
grandmothers, taken about the year 1916—she's photo-
graphed against a background of flags and Dread-
noughts. She looks astonishingly like my daughter. It's
only natural that I want to know about them. I want to
know what they were thinking and doing, and I want to
know about their general circumstances.

For most people, even now, family history comes to a
dead end about three generations back. But we are also
members of nations, and what we can't know about our
immediate ancestors we want to know about our ancestors in general. You can take the here and now just as it

is. But the moment you start asking why things are as they are, you have to investigate the past.

Why do men wear collars and ties and jackets with buttons that often don't and can't do up? It's because our own formal clothing stands in a direct line from the English and French court dress of the late seventeenth century. Why do we talk of "toeing the line?" It's because in nineteenth century state schools, children would have to stand on a chalked line to read to the class. Why does the British fiscal year for individuals start on the 6th April? It's because, until 1752, we used the Julian Calendar, which was eleven days behind the more accurate Gregorian Calendar; and the first day of the year was the 25th March. Lord Chesterfield's Act standardised us with Scotland and much of Europe, and moved the first day of the year back to January—but the fiscal year, adjusted for the new calendar, was left unchanged.

Why was Ireland, until recently, so devoutly Catholic? Because the Catholic Church was the one great institution of Irish life that could be neither abolished nor co-opted by their British rulers. Why is the Church losing its hold? Because it is no longer needed for its old purpose. The child sex scandals are only a secondary cause. History tells us who we are. We may feel trapped by it. We may glory in it. We can't ignore it.

Now, the historical novel as we know it emerged at the end of the eighteenth century. The great historians of that age—Hume, Robertson, Gibbon and others—had moved far towards what may be called a scientific study of the past. They tried to base their narratives on established fact, and to connect them through a natural relationship of cause and effect. It was a mighty achievement. At the same time, it turned History from a story book of personal encounters and the occasional miracle to something more abstract. More and more, it did away with the kind of story that you find in Herodotus and Livy and Froissart. As we move into the nineteenth century, it couldn't satisfy a growing taste for the quaint and the romantic.

The vacuum was filled by a school of historical novelists with Sir Walter Scott at its head. Though no longer much read, he was a very good novelist. *The Bride of Lammermoor* is one of his best, but has been overshadowed by the Donizetti opera. I've never met anyone else who has read *The Heart of Midlothian*. But *Ivanhoe* remains popular, and is still better than any of its adaptations. Whether still read or not, he established all the essential rules of historical fiction. The facts, so far as we can know them, are not to be set aside. They are, however, to be elaborated and folded into a coherent fictional narrative. Take *Ivanhoe*. King Richard was detained abroad. His brother, John, was a bad regent, and may not have wanted Richard back. There were rich Jews in England, and, rather than fleecing them, as the morality of his age allowed, John tried to flay them. But Ivanhoe and Isaac of York, and the narrative thread that leads to the re-emergence of King Richard at its climax—these are fiction.

I try to respect these conventions in my six Aelric novels. Aelric of England never existed. He didn't turn up in Rome in 609AD, to uncover and foil a plot that I'd rather not discuss in detail. He didn't move to Constantinople in 610, and become one of the key players in the revolution that overthrew the tyrant Phocas. He wasn't the Emperor's Legate in Alexandria a few years later. He didn't purify the Empire's silver coinage, or conceive the land reforms and cuts in taxes and government spending that stabilised the Byzantine Empire for about four hundred years. He didn't lead a pitifully small army into battle against the biggest Persian invasion of the West since Xerxes. He had nothing to do, in extreme old age, with Greek Fire. Priscus existed, and may have been a beastly as I describe him. I find it reasonable to suppose that the Emperor Heraclius was not very competent without others to advise him. But the stories are fabrications. They aren't history. They are entertainment.

Even so, they are underpinned by historical fact. The background is as nearly right as I can make it. I've read everything I could find about the age in English and French and Latin and Greek. I've read dozens of specialist works, and hundreds of scholarly articles. My *Blood of Alexandria* is a good introduction to the political and religious state of Egypt on the eve of the Arab invasions. My *Curse of Babylon* is a good introduction to the Empire as a whole in the early years of the seventh century. The only conscious inaccuracy in all six novels comes in *Terror of Constantinople*, where I appoint a new Patriarch of Constantinople several months after the actual event. I did this for dramatic effect—among much else, it let me parody Tony Blair's Diana Funeral reading— but I've felt rather bad about it ever since. This aside, any university student who uses me for background to the period that I cover will not have been defrauded.

There's nothing special about this. If you want to know about Rome between Augustus and Nero, the best place to start is the two Claudius novels by Robert Graves. Mary Renault is often as good a Grote or Bury on Classical Greece—sometimes better in her descriptions of the moral climate. Gore Vidal's *Julian* is first class historical fiction, and also sound biography. Anyone who gets no further than C.S. Forrester and Patrick O'Brien will know the Royal Navy in the age of the French Wars. Mika Waltari is less reliable on the eighteenth Dynasty in The Egyptian. In mitigation, we know very little about the events and family relationships of the age between Amenhotep III and Horemheb. He wrote a memorable novel despite its boggy underpinning of fact.

I could move from here to talking about bad historical novels. But I won't. "Judge not, lest ye be judged" is the proper text for anyone like me to bear in mind. What I will do instead is talk about some of the technical difficulties of writing historical fiction. The first is one of balance. If you write a novel about Julius Caesar or

Alexander the Great, you start with certain advantages. We all know roughly who these people were. We already have Rex Warner and Robert Graves and Mary Renault. We have all the films and television serials and documentaries. We know that Rome was a collapsing republic before it became an Empire, and that Alexander got as far as India, and died in Babylon. Everyone has heard of Cicero and Aristotle. It's the same with novels set in the Second World War, or the reign of Elizabeth I. You can give the occasional spot of background, but largely get on with the narrative.

When I chose the early seventh century, I ran straight into difficulties of balancing narrative and background. The average English-speaking reader doesn't know what happened after the "fall" of Rome in the fifth century. The general view is that the Empire was overwhelmed by a flood of barbarians, after which we jump over a "dark age" to novels about Alfred the Great. There is some awareness of a continuing Empire in the East, ruled from Constantinople. But Byzantine history has always been a minority interest. There's so much of it, and little of it connects with our own past. You simply can't expect your readers to know any of the details of the seventh century, especially as they were seen from Constantinople.

Without giving readers a great deal of the background in depth, the novels would be incomprehensible. In *Conspiracies of Rome*, for example, Aelric arrives in a Rome that has no Emperor, but is still part of the Empire. There are still Senators, but no Senate. The Pope is the effective power, but is formally subordinate to a Byzantine Governor in Ravenna. Much of Italy is ruled by the Lombards, but there is a long strip of Imperial territory connecting Rome to Ravenna. Though ruined and depopulated, the Rome of the Emperors maintains a ghostly existence. Add to this that Aelric blunders right into the high politics of the Empire. The average reader needs some guidance here.

51

On the other hand, this is a first person narrative. The pretence is that Aelric is writing in old age for an audience that may not be entirely familiar with the details of Rome when he was there, but that is also not ignorant of the basics of how to wipe your bottom, or what the Arian Heresy was about. Endless lecturing digressions would distance readers from narrator, and would clog an otherwise tight narrative structure.

I don't think I got the balance entirely right in *Conspiracies*. I do better in the other five novels. But the general answer is to work out the minimum needed to make sense of the story, and to give it to the reader through dialogue and action. Once you get into the right habits, you can pack a lot of information into the actual plot development. I won't make outrageous claims for my talent as a writer. I am, however, pleased with the technical solutions I found to this problem.

The second difficulty is language. Older historical novelists often had a taste for ludicrous dialogue—"'Get thee hence,' cried the King. 'Before one moon shall have passed, thou must bring me the head of the false Rutland!" *etc*, *etc*. Every age has its own tastes, but this doesn't work now. When people spoke to each other in the past, they sounded natural to each other. Making them speak Shakespearese devalues your characters. If your novel is set in the eighteenth century, you can try for real authenticity. But this is hard to get right, and your readers will struggle with whatever colloquial speech you reconstruct from court records and letters. The best approach—used by Patrick O'Brien, for example—is to give dialogue a faintly Augustan intonation, but otherwise to avoid obvious modernisms.

I don't have this problem in my Aelric novels. The pretence throughout is that Aelric is writing his memoirs in Greek, and these have been translated into idiomatic modern English. From about the second to the nineteenth centuries, Greek writers would, unless they were trying to be grand, skip between classical and demotic usages according to their need. Therefore, I do the same in English—mixing Augustanism with modern vulgarity. Take this as an example from my *Curse of Babylon*:

> But all that could wait. Lucas was waiting outside the walls, and with evidence that might let me save still more of the taxpayers' money on salaries and pensions. I prepared to hurry down into Imperial Square.
>
> 'Might Your Honour be a gambling man?' someone asked in the wheedling tone of the poor. I paid no attention and looked up at the sky—not a cloud in sight, but the gathering shift to a northern wind would soon justify my blue woollen cloak. 'Go on, Sir—I can see it's your lucky day!' I looked round at someone with the thin and wiry build of the working lower classes. He looked under the brim of my hat and laughed. 'For you, Sir, I'll lay special odds,' he said. 'You drop any coin you like in that bowl down there.' I didn't follow his pointed finger. I'd already seen the disused fountain thirty feet below in Imperial Square. He put his face into a snarling grin. 'Even a gold coin you can drop, Sir. The ten foot of green slime don't count for nothing with my boy. He'll jump right off this wall beside you, and get it out for you.'
>
> I was about to tell him to bugger off and die, when I looked at the naked boy who'd come out from behind a column. I felt a sudden stirring of lust. Like all the City's lower class, he was a touch undersized and there was a slight lack of harmony in the proportion of his legs to his body. For all this, his tanned skin was rather fetching. Give him a bath and...
>
> Oh dear! He'd no sooner got me thinking of how much to offer, when he swept the hair from his eyes and parted very full lips to show two rows of rotten teeth. The front ones were entirely gone. The others were blackened stumps. Such a shame! Such a waste! So little beauty there was already in this world—and why did so much of that have to be spoiled? I could have thrashed the boy's owner for not making him clean every day with a chewing stick. I wrinkled my

nose and stood up.

His owner hadn't noticed. 'Oh, Sir, Sir!' he cried, getting directly in my way and waving his arms to stop me. 'Sir, the deal is this. You throw in a coin. If the boy gets it out, you pay me five times your coin. If he can't find it, I pay you five times. If he breaks his neck or drowns, I pay you ten times.' He laughed and pointed at the boy again. I didn't look, but wondered if I might make an exception. Bad teeth are bad teeth—but the rest of him was pushing towards excellent.

But I shook my head. I could fuck anything I wanted later in the day. Until then, duty was calling me again. Trying not to show I was running away, I hurried down the steps. [Chapter 8]

I think this does the job. It sounds natural. The incident isn't a diversion from the plot: the boy comes in handy later on. It also gives something of the social background. I'll have to let the readers decide.

What is it about the Classical Era that led you to writing your novels in that time?

Another big question. I discovered the Greeks when I was eight, and I came across a copy of Roger Lancelyn-Green's retelling of *The Iliad*. I was smitten at once. There was something so wonderfully grand, yet exotic, about the stories. I didn't get very far with it, but I found a copy of *Teach Yourself Greek* in the local library and spent weeks puzzling over it. Over the next few years, I read my way through the whole of Greek and Roman mythology, and was drawn into the history of the whole ancient world.

When I was twelve, my classical leanings took me in a new, if wholly predictable, direction. The sexual revolution of the 1970s hardly touched most South London schoolboys. The one sex education lesson I had was a joke. Porn was whatever I could see without my glasses in the swimming pool. So I taught myself Latin well enough to read the untranslated naughty bits in the Loeb editions of the classics. The librarians in Lewisham were very particular in those days about what they allowed on their shelves. They never questioned the prestige of the classics, or thought about what I was getting them to order in from other libraries. With help from Martial and Suetonius and Ausonius, among others, I'd soon worked out the mechanics of all penetrative sex, and flagellation and depilation and erotic dances; and I had a large enough fund of anecdotes and whole stories to keep my imagination at full burn all though puberty.

Then, as I grew older, I realised something else about the Greeks—something I'd always known without putting it into words. There's no doubt that European civilisation, at least since the Renaissance, has outclassed every other. No one ever gathered facts like we do. No one reasoned from them more profoundly or with greater focus. No one approached us in exposing the forces of nature, and in turning them to human advantage. We are now four or five centuries into a curve of progress that keeps turning more steeply upwards. Yet our first steps were guided by others—the Greek, the Romans, the Arabs, and so forth. If we see further than they do, we stand on the backs of giants.

The Greeks had no one to guide them. Unless you want to make exaggerated claims about the Egyptians and Phoenicians, they began from nothing. Between about 600 and 300 BC, the Greeks of Athens and some of the cities of what is now the Turkish coast were easily the most remarkable people who ever lived. They gave us virtually all our philosophy, and the foundation of all our sciences. Their historians were the finest. Their poetry was second only to that of Homer—and it was they who put together all that we have of Homer. They gave us ideals of beauty, the fading of which has always been a warning sign of decadence; and they gave us the technical means of recording that beauty. Again, they had no examples to imitate. They did everything entirely by themselves. In a world that had always been at the midnight point of barbarism and superstition, they went off like a flashbulb; and everything good in our own world is part of their afterglow. Every renaissance and enlightenment we have had since then has begun with a rediscovery of the ancient Greeks. Modern chauvinists may argue whether England or France or Germany has given more to the world. In truth, none of us is fit to kiss the dust on which the ancient Greeks walked.

How can you stumble into their world, and not eventually be astonished by what the Greeks achieved? From the time I was eight, into early manhood, I felt wave after wave of adoration wash over me, each one more powerful than the last.

Even so, from my first reading of Gibbon, I was also drawn towards the very end of Antiquity—the series of crises that began in the third century, and that, by about 650, shattered the fabric of ancient civilisation. When it came to writing my first historical novel, I could easily have set it in Classical Athens, or in Rome under Tiberius or Domitian. Instead, I chose the end period. The idea first came early in 2004, when my wife took me for a long weekend in Rome. It was a bitterly cold four days in February, and we wandered round the Forum and the remains of the Imperial Palace, and the Coliseum and all the museums. But I found myself more powerfully drawn to the fourth and fifth century churches, and buildings and inscriptions from the early middle ages. These are buildings that haven't fallen down, and that give a strong sense of continuity with the past. I kept asking myself what it was like to be in Rome when these buildings were new, and the grander buildings from the Imperial age were still standing, though falling into ruin.

The result was *Conspiracies of Rome*, which I wrote quickly in 2005, and then put away. When it came out in 2008, it was an immediate success, and five more followed. I still worship the Classical Greeks. But my last visit to Turkey saw me among the ruins of Aphrodisias and Hierapolis almost out of duty. My biggest thrill is to walk though the bronze doors recycled from a temple in Ephesus into the Great Church in Constantinople. The Turks conquered Byzantium fair and square, and Islam is their faith. It would be a terrible thing, even so, if they turned the place back into a mosque and covered over the mosaics again. Writing the Aelric novels has turned me into something of a Byzantine patriot!

It's widely thought that sexuality in the Classical Era was much more fluid in comparison to modern Western thinking (or rather, before recent developments). Do you feel that your stories are in keeping with how society thought at the time, or do you write with a message in mind for today's society?

There are two opposed beliefs about sexuality in the ancient world. Both are false, though not equally so. The first is that the ancient world fizzled out in an orgy of bum fun, and that we need to be careful not to let this happen to us. Where do you begin with a belief so completely unfounded on the evidence? I suppose you look to the evidence. Alexander the Great and Julius Caesar both had a taste for all-male sex. So did Mark Antony. So did Hadrian. So had most of the famous Athenians—Euripides being one of its most notable enthusiasts. No signs there of moral or any other weakness. If Mark Antony came to a bad end, it was because he married an ambitious foreign woman.

A growing prejudice against all-male sex becomes visible in the fourth century, when Constantine established Christianity as the official faith. He made the first laws against it. Within a century, the Goths were across the Rhine and had sacked Rome. Oh, and one of Constantine's own sons had a taste for Gothic boys!

It's absurd to try correlating national greatness or decline with sexual customs. Ancient civilisation didn't collapse because its rulers were too worn out from buggering each other to take up swords. The ultimate cause may have been a mild global cooling, which lowered the Malthusian ceiling. There was an undoubted growth of rural impoverishment that left populations open to the pandemic diseases that swept through the Mediterranean world from late in the second century. Population decline was then worsened by various forms of misgovernment, and by the need to hold frontiers that had only made sense in an age of economic and demographic expansion. Rather than bursting through in unstoppable floods, the barbarians seem eventually to have wandered, in small bands, into a demographic vacuum.

The second false belief is that the ancient world was one big al fresco bath house. I once watched a television documentary in which it was seriously maintained that straight sex was out of fashion in Athens during the classical period. I thought of writing in to ask what books the researchers had been reading.

Because it lasted over a thousand years, and flourished on three continents, you should be careful about generalisations about ancient civilisation. But one good generalisation is that free men were expected to marry and beget children. These were societies with high death rates. They needed high birth rates not to die out. They particularly needed large numbers of young men to fight in their endemic wars of conquest or survival. Those men who wouldn't breed were sometimes punished. Those who couldn't were expected to adopt the surplus children of their poorer friends and relatives.

There were also strong prejudices against men who took the passive role in oral and anal sex. Take, for example, this epigram somewhere in Martial:

> *Secti podicis usque ad umbilicum*
> *Nullas reliquias habet Charinus*
> *Et prurit tamen usque ad umbilicum.*
> *O quanta scabie miser laborat:*
> *Culum non habet, est tamen cinaedus.*

> *[Of his anus, split right up to the belly button,*
> *Nothing remains to Charinus.*
> *And still he longs for it right up to his belly button.*

58

O behold the poor dear's itching:
No arse left, yet still he longs to be fucked.]

On the other hand, the ancients didn't have our concept of gay and straight. Latin has a large and precise sexual vocabulary—though you won't find meanings in the standard dictionaries. See, for example: *Irrumator*, one who presents his penis for sucking; *Fellator*, one who sucks; *Pathicus*, the passive partner in anal sex, *Exoletus*, the active partner; *Cinaedus*, a male prostitute; *Catamitus*, a boy prostitute or lover; *Glabrarius*, lover of smooth-skinned boys; *Tribas*, a woman with a clitoris large enough to serve as a penis—and so it continues. The Greek vocabulary is larger still. There is no word in either language that means "homosexual." *Sodomitus* is a late word, brought in by the Christians, and may not have had its present meaning until deep into the middle ages.

So long as legitimate children were somehow begotten, and so long as he didn't disgrace himself by taking the passive role, what else a free man did was legally and morally indifferent. Elsewhere in his works, Martial boasts of sleeping with boys, and scolds his wife for thinking ill of him. In Athens and some other classical city states, it was a social duty for men in the higher classes to have sexual affairs with adolescent boys. We all know about the Spartans. In Thebes, an army was formed of adult sex partners. If anyone had said that all-male sex was in itself wrong, he'd have been laughed at. The Jews, who did say this, were despised. The Christian Emperors may have made laws against it. They were mostly enforced against political enemies when no other charges were credible or convenient.

Indeed, while there was a prejudice, and sometimes laws, against sexual passivity, it's obvious that, once in private, men did as they pleased. One of the fundamental rules of the man-boy affairs in Athens was no anal penetration and no fellatio. Sex was supposed to involve mutual masturbation or intercrural friction. You can imagine how that rule was kept in private. There were problems only if the truth got out. Philip of Macedon, for example, kept a boy as his lover. One day, in public, he poked the boy in the stomach and asked why he wasn't yet pregnant. The boy was so outraged that he murdered the King.

Then we have slavery, and the total power of an owner over his slaves. A slave-owner could demand whatever he liked, and expect the world not to be told about what he liked. So long as they weren't physically injured, slaves were universally expected to do as they were told and not complain. As for prostitution, Rome and the larger cities were filled with brothels offering every sexual act imaginable. When Bible quotes failed, Christians were warned away from the brothels on the grounds that they might accidentally sleep with their own abandoned and enslaved children.

I haven't mentioned all-female sex. Nor, though, did most ancient writers. Everyone knows about Sappho. But we are more interested in her sexuality than any of the ancient critics. At best, the surviving writings about her deal with her tastes in casual asides, and only to explain the meaning of her text. This may seem curious. Women are at least as inclined to have sex with each other as men with each other—and human nature doesn't change much in its fundamentals between different times and places. And the ancients were hardly reticent about sex. The reason, I think, is that, for the ancients, sex wasn't sex unless an ejaculating penis was somewhere involved. Nothing else counted.

Let me cite another of Martial's epigrams. This one is about a woman called Philaenis. In other epigrams, she is called lusca—that is, she has only one eye. In this one, she is called *tribas*—again, a woman with a very large clitoris. The opening lines go:

Paedicat pueros tribas Philaenis

Et tentigine saevior mariti
Undenas dolat in die puellas....

[Philaenis buggers boys,
And, crueller than a lustful bridegroom,
Deflowers eleven girls a day....]

As with the lines about Charinus, you could take this out of context as a sneer against same-sex intercourse. Martial ridicules Philaenis, though, not because she has sex with girls, but because she has abandoned the role assigned her by Nature, and is behaving like a man. Note how he begins with her apparently equal taste for sex with boys. This is not an anti-lesbian work, but an assertion of gender stereotypes. Later in the epigram, he takes issue with her taste for exercising in the gymnasium. Women were not supposed to behave like men. Whatever else they did—so long, of course, as it did not involve the wrong penis—wasn't worth discussing. It seems that husbands didn't regard lesbian affairs as adultery. It may also be that they weren't worried if their women had sex with eunuchs—who were often cut late enough to be capable of erection and orgasm, though not to be capable of disgracing a man with bastard children.

The ancients were often more liberal about sex than we are. But they were not generally more liberal. They were governed by prejudices quite as strong as our own. But they were different prejudices. If they didn't care about the gender of sexual partners, they were obsessed by many of the attendant circumstances.

The lead character to your novels is clearly bisexual. What was your reasoning behind this?

See above for a general answer. Aelric is young and beautiful, and increasingly rich and powerful. He's clever and is honest about his tastes. He despises religion, and puts up with Christianity only because nearly everyone else believes in it, and because it may be politically useful. Of course, he's bisexual. Given the continuing moral climate of his world, what else should he be? It wasn't a matter any normal man would think about. In Curse of Babylon, he's in love with Antonia. But he's also in love with two of his dancing boys—who adore him in return, and who turn into ruthless killers, reckless of their own safety, when he needs their help. Antonia doesn't object. She forms her own semi-maternal relationship with one of the boys. Why should she be jealous? She's the one who will marry Aelric and bear the children. She might think differently about a female concubine. Ancient sexuality was constrained more by considerations of status and honour than by the teachings of Levitcus and St Paul.

Tell us a bit about the latest book; what can readers expect, and how different is it from your previous works?

If you've read any of the others, *Curse of Babylon* gives you more of the same—though perhaps a little more of some things. According to *The Morning Star*, I give readers "a near-perfect blend of historical detail and atmosphere with the plot of a conspiracy thriller, vivid characters, high philosophy and vulgar comedy." I won't say if the blend is near-perfect, but that is what I try to produce. Another reviewer has called me "the Ken Russell of historical fiction." I don't think this was meant to be a compliment, but I'll take it as one. Though I try for naturalism of speech and action, I also manage a lurid, Technicolor gloss. You'll see all this in *Curse*. It has kidnaps and daring escapes, blood and sex everywhere, acrobatic fights that owe much to Hollywood at its best, and a gigantic battle at the climax.

Now, you do ask about politics. The trouble about political novels of any ideology is that they too often veer across the border between entertainment and propaganda. But I am an ideologue, and this shows through in my fiction. I believe that government is, in itself, a bad thing, and that most other bad things are made worse by government. The world would be a better place without all the vast structures of control that now constrain our lives. I hope you will see this belief in my fiction. I also hope it doesn't hit you over the head.

Review Article, Acts of Destruction

Acts of Destruction
Mat Coward
Alia Mondo Press, Norwich, 2009, 264pp, £10.00, pb
ISBN is 978-1-4401-6322-7
Available via Amazon or from *www.matcoward.com*

Acts of Destruction is a semi-humorous crime novel set about twenty years into the future. Its underlying premise is that shortages of oil and other raw materials put an end, after about 2010, to the global economic order as we presently know it. The United States collapses into a predictable mix of centralised fascism and armed separatism. The European Union avoids the full horrors of America, but turns inward and becomes more overtly authoritarian and state capitalist. The British response, however, is to reset the political and economic clock to 1945, and to complete all the unfinished business of the Atlee Government.

In Mr Coward's Britain of about 2030, a new constitution called "The Agreement of the People" has collectivised the economy and radically decentralised politics. Most government is local and controlled by direct democracy. The remaining central government is balanced by strong localism and by frequent referenda. At every level, there is an obsessive regard for procedural fairness and transparency, and for many kinds of personal freedom. Increasing numbers of people work in collective enterprises. Self-employment is tolerated, as are larger private enterprises that do not employ more than fifty people, or are not engaged in work of patriotic importance. People grow much of their own food. Many other things are rationed. Most transport is public, and everything is recycled. In a generally awful world, Britain has managed to become a country at peace with itself. It preserves its independence by an armed citizen militia.

It would be dishonest for me to pass over this scenario and move straight to a discussion of the plot and the technical quality of its narrative. In more ways that one, reading *Acts of Destruction* was a trip down Memory Lane. Almost every second page, I found myself looking up to recall the old libertarian analysis of socialism that I last set out at length before the end of the Cold War and the emergence of new threats to liberty. I will not make this review into an economic tract, but I do feel the need to make some comment.

The Britain described by Mr Coward is impossible. Without markets and market pricing, there can be no economic coordination except through a rigid structure of command. Even this will be starved of necessary information. Individual preferences and valuations are always subjective, and usually unspoken, and they can change from moment to moment. It is the same with knowledge of where to find things and what to do with them. No planning authority is capable of gathering and updating and using such information. Actual coordination must rely on the preferences and valuations and knowledge either of a planning committee or of a still smaller group to which the committee reports. Except in the most formal and probably illusory sense, there can be no room for democratic supervision. Democratic or decentralised economic planning is as much an impossibility as expecting several hundred participatory soldier committees to have organised the D Day Landings. There are things that must be done and not done. There is a necessary balance between the things that must be done, and a correct sequence in which they must be done. To avoid chaos, whoever is planning an economy must have reasonably despotic control over activity—control that is not democratically unaccountable, save perhaps after the event, and not subject to the normal rule of law.

Moreover, unless a community is fighting a war of

survival or coping with an overpowering natural disaster, many planning decisions will be opposed. Because local knowledge cannot be taken into account, they will also be perceived as inefficient—and will be actually inefficient in terms of measurable output and quality of output. Direction will, therefore, need some kind of police state to ensure obedience to apparently meaningless or perverse orders. This will be accompanied by lies about the wisdom and goodness of those in charge, and by more or less hysterical campaigns against foreign or domestic saboteurs. Forget about the headline promises in Mr Coward's Agreement of the People, and the formality of local democracy. The reality of his future Britain would have to be mass-poverty, administrative corruption and brutality, and a ruling class able, and eventually willing, to arrange lives of secret luxury for its own members.

Add to this that Mr Coward's Britain is noticeably multi-racial—though not, it seems, multicultural. People of different races can live together in peace in two kinds of political arrangement. They can live under a government that has no economic privileges to hand out, and that does not interfere in matters of religion or education or private life. Or they can live under a government that has ruthlessly terrorised every self-defined group out of existence, and rules over a mass of atomised individuals. Mr Coward's political arrangement will bring about all the evils described above, within a territory filled with competing ethnic mafias.

The standard reply to this critique is to insist that socialism will create a "new man" with different and more noble motivations. But I see no reason in the abstract why this should happen; and our actual experience of mid-twentieth century collectivism provided no evidence to the contrary.

This is the limit of my critique. Though it has to be stated I see no reason to carry it any further. On the one hand, the sort of collectivism von Mises and Hayek did so much to analyse is unlikely to be tried again. On the other, I am reviewing a novel, not responding to a socialist manifesto. This being said, I will proceed with my review.

For me, the main excellence of *Acts of Destruction* is its technical skill. I have written an alternative history novel, involving a Britain radically different from Mr Coward's own utopia. I have written a post-apocalyptic novel set in a Britain that is also radically different from Mr Coward's. I have also written half a dozen historical novels set in an age of which most of my readers know hardly anything. Each time, I have faced the challenge of how to explain the background to my narrative. This is a challenge that readers do not generally notice, but how it is met by a writer largely determines whether he can be regarded as a competent novelist. There are, broadly speaking, three ways of meeting the challenge. You can interrupt the narrative with long authorial digressions. You can make your characters speak to each other in pamphletese. Or you can integrate all necessary information about background into the narrative.

Let me illustrate these various approaches. Here is an example of the first:

> It was now thirty years after the repulse of the alien invasion. The sudden and apparently total unity of the human race created by the first Vegan attack did not long survive the destruction of their Death Star. Within months, Jews and Arabs were back to arguing about Palestine. The Indians and Pakistanis were marching up and down their disputed borders. The British remained semi-detached Europeans. The Americans were once more preaching their own version of "human rights" to people who neither understood nor desired what was on offer. Men still murdered their wives for the insurance money. Conmen still robbed old ladies of their life savings.
>
> At the same time, the vaporising of every large city, and the need for every able-bodied adult to be trusted with weapons, had brought lasting changes to the

lifestyle and the moral outlook of humanity….

Here is an example of the second:

John looked up from his newspaper. "It was necessary to kill them all," he said flatly.

Janet poured another cup of tea, and seemed unwilling to respond. Then: "I still don't like the way our parents' generation rounded them up and dissolved them in the sea. At least, we could have spared the young in their cocoons. Could we not have studied them? They are the only alien life forms we have encountered. We could have learnt so much."

"No!" John shouted, banging the table. "As Generalissimo Patel said, 'Kindness to the enemy is treason to ourselves.' Once we had discovered their weakness, we had time for only one strike. The world of competing nation states and races and religions that our children once more see as natural and inevitable may not be perfect. But can you imagine the possible consequences of allowing one strand of Vegan DNA to remain in being once Carmichael and Shitzu had made their desperate and suicidal attack on the Death Star?"

It was time for John to set out for the office….

Here is an example of the third:

The old man was looking shifty again. "I don't know what you're talking about," he muttered.

I smiled and lit a cigarette. "Look, Mr Trimble," I began in a more reasonable tone of voice, "of course I know the history of the War, and I have your military record in front of me." I stabbed the forefinger of my left hand at the tablet screen. I waited for the relevant paragraph to enlarge. "The big counterattack began on the 3rd October 2022, and you were one of the first men into the liberated holding camp outside Leicester. It was messy stuff, and you don't have to go into the details of what you found in the Vegan implantation centre." I leaned forward. Not speaking, I continued by putting each word one at a time in my own head. "My question is how a bullet fired from your rifle found its way into Professor Sanderson's back, and what you were doing alone for fifteen minutes in the transmuting room."

For just the tiniest moment, he failed to conceal that he'd read my mind....

The first method is entirely legitimate. It was used extensively by Walter Scott and by Disraeli, to name only two classic writers who come to mind. It was used by Isaac Asimov. I used it myself in my first historical novel, and had no choice but to use it for geographical information in my latest. It can be overused. It then slows down the narrative, and tends to make the characters into something like the figures in a tableau. The second is hardly ever legitimate. People do not speak in this way. As given above, it is the sure sign of an incompetent writer. I sometimes use a modified form in my historical novels, but only where the whole drift of a conversation allows one of the characters to start a lecture. In one novel, I let my narrator explain something complex to an illiterate slave who needs to be put in the know. It cut out the need for pages of military and political narrative. In another, my narrator is answering a child's questions. This let me give a potted account of the Persian and Islamic wars in seventh century Byzantium. Even so, it is a method that must be sparingly used. Once again, it can slow down the narrative.

The third method is the best, and you can sweat for hours over a single paragraph to make the giving of information sound natural. No synoptic account of your world will ever be given. The account emerges instead from a reading of what your characters say and do. Some things will not be explained at all. Others will be compared to things outside your reader's imagination that still say something about your world—for example: "It was about the size of a self-charging television battery." This is Mr Coward's preferred method, and it shows either a natural talent for narrative, or—more likely—great care and labour. Take this:

When Greg, Catherine and four local uniformed officers arrived to serve their search warrant, they found the McFarlanes watching TV coverage of the final ODI between Afghanistan and Britain, live from Edinburgh.

"We were expecting a visit from the police," Alicia McFarland told Greg, "but we weren't expecting a search warrant."

"I'm sorry about that, but it was a necessary precaution. I'm sure the officers will be careful to return everything to its proper place."

"They'd better be," said Andrew McFarlane, with what Catherine took to be an attempt at a brave smile for his wife. "I know most of their parents." [p.125]

What you have here is four paragraphs of mixed action and dialogue that both advance the narrative and explain the background. If you read nothing else in the novel, you see the nature of Mr Coward's utopia.

The story itself is unremarkable. It is a tale of everyday policing in a world somewhat different from our own. The police are investigating two murders and a missing child. There is also a series of thefts from factory rooftop gardens, and a cartload of junk that has not been recycled but dumped into a flood pond. Calling the story unremarkable is not a criticism. My own taste in plots is rather more spectacular: I write under the joint influence of French grand opera and Hollywood science fiction of the 1980s. In *Acts of Destruction*, I might wish that the capitalist conspiracy had been woven deeper into the main plot. I certainly think that Austin Molloy, the American refugee, could have been given a bigger role and made more sinister. For me, the novel does lack a villain. But there is an advantage in keeping to the more prosaic side of life in a socialist utopia. It makes everything more real—and, I will confess, more attractive.

I come back to the politics of the novel. I repeat that Mr Coward's utopia is a dream that falls to pieces the moment any tool of economic or political analysis is applied to it. It strikes me, though, as a jolly place in which to be alive—rather better than our own sub-Orwellian nightmare state. I dislike the idea of locking rifles away when not used for militia practice—better, though, than a having a population of disarmed and therefore terrified sheep. I dislike the idea of licensed prostitution and licensed production of recreational drugs—better, though, than attempts at prohibition. I dislike the idea of compulsory purchase of any business with more than fifty employees—better, though, than the virtual ban we have on self-employment for the poor and unskilled. I dislike the idea of any curbs on religious proselytism, and there is no offset here. Then again, I do appreciate Mr Coward's full libertarianism on other issues. Even his female characters smoke pipes. The authorities encourage pubs and communal drinking. And here is Mr Coward on the health fascists:

> "At one point," said Catherine [in the bad old days], "some schools banned Marmite, because it was considered too salty."

> "They banned Marmite?" For Erin, it seemed, an interesting historical discussion had just become personal.

> "Marmite." Catherine nodded. "On the same list as switchblades and heroin."

> "That's right," said Bob. "It all became very competitive—who could go farthest, either as an individual, or corporately."

> "Yeah, but why did the government get involved?"

> "I think it goes back to the 1980s," said Catherine. "There was this new ideology that said that governments shouldn't interfere with running the country. All that—the economy, housing, jobs, even health and education—to the free market to sort out. But of course, government still existed, we still had politicians. They just didn't have anything to do—everything had been privatised."

"But they had to do something all day other than snooze," said Bob. "And nature abhors a vacuum, so they devoted themselves full-time to telling people what they could and couldn't eat, how much of each food they were allowed per day…" [p.237]

He makes a fair point. Ministers who were up to their ears in trying to run the railway network, and persuade the coal miners not to go on strike, never found the time to tell us whether and where we could smoke, or how much salt to put in our boiled potatoes. My only disagreement is that the modest and temporary retreat of the British State in the 1980s should have been accompanied by systematic cuts to the apparatus of government. Politicians should control neither the railways nor our diets. But, if I had to choose, social democracy is better than micromanagement of our lives. Nationalised railways usually work well enough. Even the National Union of Mineworkers could be jollied into digging out coal most of the time.

Indeed, the main trip down Memory Lane that I mention is the sense of return to an age that I am just old enough to have seen at its end. This was the age that opened in May 1940 and faded away a few years before or after the 1979 election. When I was a boy, men wore hats. They often wore ties at home. They smoked without any sense of guilt or alarm. They were restrained in their language, and easy in their relationships with women and children. Most inequality of income was within a narrow band, and it was expected that this band would continue narrowing. Nearly everyone felt secure in his job. The word "unemployment" conjured up black and white images of men in flat caps and with no back teeth.

Like every other good Tory boy, I railed against the Atlee Settlement as if we were on the verge of Stalin's Russia. There were problems. We had a second rate political class, unable to balance the budget and establish a stable place in the world, given the decline of our relative national power. We had a largely third rate business class, unable to provide decent goods and services and to deal with a trade union movement that was rightly suspicious of its competence. Because of flaws in the Keynesian and Beveridge scheme of things, I think the whole system was doomed in the long run. Looking back, though, it had much to recommend it. More than that—it was the best time in all of British history to be alive.

Imagine you could go back to about 1965 and bring forward an intelligent man in his forties. Show him round modern Britain. No doubt, he would be astonished by the wonderful electronic toys we can all have, and by our gigantic shopping centres. Then describe to him how, a year after his death, the headstone was pulled off Jimmy Savile's grave, ground smooth of its inscription, and then smashed up for landfill—all because the man may have touched up some slightly underage girls a generation earlier. Show him the endlessly revolving scares about child sex abuse and global warming, and speech codes that do nothing to help their stated beneficiaries, and much to shut down debate. Tell him that, while the Soviet Union eventually collapsed without raising a hand against us, we cower in fear before the formal or informal rulers of places like Afghanistan and Yemen, and that we fight our wars with them by sending unpiloted aeroplanes to bomb women and children. Explain to him how, one after the other, our industries were taxed or regulated out of existence, and that the children of those who used to work in them are—if lucky—now employed as casual skivvies, or as minor functionaries of a vast and out of control regulatory state.

Do all this, and your friend from the 1960s will soon feel nostalgic for his Post Office telephone and bad coffee, and for cars without air conditioning. Equally, I think the great majority of people in this country would, if given copies of *Acts of Destruction*, wish that Mr Coward's utopia could be made possible. Many, I have no doubt, would be prepared to take a chance on its possibility.

Now, something comparable is possible, though not currently on any mainstream agenda. There must be market pricing and competition. The State must leave people alone in all their choices. There must be no attempts at economic direction—no belief in a stable trade off between unemployment and inflation, or nonsensical talk of aggregate demand and multiplier effects. But co-operatives, and personal dignity, and a broad equality, and a revival of genuine communities—these are entirely consistent with a freed market. Much local production would probably flourish in a world without transport and infrastructure subsidies, and wars to subdue or stabilise foreign markets. Freed of a choice between life as a "human resource" in some global corporation and rotting on the dole, people would feel secure enough to stand up for their legal rights and to protect those of their neighbours. So long as it does not encourage parasitism, and can be made self-liquidating with the increase of wealth, there is even some room for state welfare. The world as we have it is not the only possible type of capitalism. It is not even a place of reasonably free markets.

The great failing of the libertarian movement—certainly in this country, almost certainly also in America—has been its partiality to corporatist big business. I think, for example, of organisations like the Adam Smith Institute. For a third of a century, it has shamefully used libertarian rhetoric to justify abominations like the Poll Tax and the Private Finance Initiative, and privatisations that have been little more than transfers of privileged monopolies from state to formally private ownership. Much of the reason for this is that the movement has been dominated by intermediaries between privilege-hunting businessmen and well-intentioned but mercenary writers. Otherwise, it is filled with men the foresight of whose parents allows them to participate in the market purely as consumers, or with men who are doing well in one of the City casinos, and who think they have

74

earned their wealth by untrammelled market exchanges. Not surprisingly, the growing immiserisation of the working classes is ignored or seen as a moral failing of the people affected.

The kindest judgment anyone can pass on traditional socialism is that it was tried and it failed. Even the mixed economy welfare state in which I grew up was unsustainable, and would have been with much better management. But there is nothing ignoble or inaccurate about the moral outrage that gave socialism its hold over the imagination. At all times and in every place, ruling classes have behaved badly to those under them, and they have always been largely or wholly unnecessary. It would be nice if, in his future novels, Mr Coward could join his denunciations of the present with a more accurate analysis of why it is so bad, and of how it can be made better. It would be nice if, instead of speaking in terms of "left" and "right," and attacking each other for what we may not actually have said, we could all speak simply of "us" and "them."

But this takes me beyond my review of a novel that I heartily commend to anyone who likes original and thoughtful and well-constructed fiction. *Acts of Destruction* deserves to be read far beyond the socialist movement for which it was written.

Review Article, Sword of Marathon

Sword of Marathon
By Jack England
Published August 2012
ISBN: 978 14781

The hero of this novel is an Englishman of great intelligence and beauty who settles in Greece. He begins telling his story in extreme old age, and, though aged, nearly has to kill someone in the first chapter. Much of the novel takes place in Athens. However, anyone who thinks the author has been influenced by my own *Ghosts of Athens* will be wrong. Jack told me he was writing *Sword of Marathon* in May 2011, when we were both attending a conference in Bodrum. I had just finished Ghosts of Athens, though it would not be published until August 2012. By then, Jack had finished *Sword of Marathon*, and was working on a sequel. There is a similarity between our novels, but I do swear that neither of us could have had any influence on the other. This really is one of those times when great minds have thought alike.

The story begins when Luke and his brother Hal are on a trading mission and are captured by nomadic and more than usually demented barbarians. Through a series of exciting and well-paced adventures, they arrive in Athens in 490, just when Darius of Persia has finally decided to have his revenge on a city that has not only resisted his invitation to accept him as overlord, but has consistently made trouble along the western fringes of the greatest empire so far to exist.

Embraced by the Athenians as one of their own, Luke plays a key part in the victorious defence of Greece against the first Persian assault, and ends the story covered in well-deserved glory.

Rather than explain in detail what I like about the

novel, let me quote this passage from when Luke and Hal are taken prisoner by the barbarians:

> The horsemen dismounted noisily at a large circular wicker hut, then pulled the two boys off their horse; they unroped Luke and Hal from each other, then bound each boy's hands tightly behind his back, before pushing them into the hut.
>
> A stench of rotting entrails filled the space, from an indeterminate set of slaughtered beasts. A wide circular pit, twelve feet across, with vertical sides, occupied most of the space inside the hut, with a post standing beside its lip, which had a long length of rope coiled around it.
>
> Instead of using the rope, the Gerroians threw both boys into the pit together, where they fell and splashed into five feet of stinking water, twisting knees and ankles when their feet crashed into mud at the pit's bottom. Luke could hear laughter and mutual back slaps amongst the men above. The group of horse-riding captors left the hut. From the floor of the pit, to the lip at the top, was at least ten feet above the surface of the water. This was an old well, thought Luke, but clearly not used for drinking water.
>
> The last man out rattled shut the hut's flimsy door, then the sound of happy men receded. Ordinary sounds of town life re-filled the hut through the wicker walls; chickens squawked, dogs barked, and domestic arguments all flowed in, along with the smells of cooked meat and wood smoke.
>
> In the bottom of the pit the boys stood up and could feel hard objects in the putrid mud under their feet. Almost drowning himself, and at risk of dislocating his shoulders, Luke managed to bring his hands around to his front.
>
> He delved into the stinking mud with his hands and brought to the surface a human skull. The top had been sliced off and there were the telltale signs of a heavy axe blow, to mark the remains of what was left. This pit involved death; that much was clear.

The author has done with this passage exactly what a competent writer does. He clearly imagines a situation, even down to the sounds of normality beyond the confines of its horror. He does this through the perceptions of his hero, leaving nothing to objective description.

Or take this:

> ...Miltiades spat up in the face of Hippias. Thick stinking phlegm dribbled down the former tyrant's lips and dripped onto his purple silks, though Hippias stayed motionless.

> "So you thought you would walk into Athens again with the same fucking plan your demented father lucked into all those years ago," said Miltiades. "Did you think we would forget, you arrogant piece of dog shit? Did you think we would run from these fucking Persian bastards and these cock-sucking Median cuts?"...

> Miltiades punched Hippias in the face and knocked out several loose blackened teeth, which created a putrid cloud of rotten breath, as bits of partially-digested meat and gristle came out with them. The teeth flew overboard, in a blood-and-spittle rain, mostly into the brackish lagoon water, though one rotten tooth fell onto the exposed sandbar that had trapped the trireme....(p.230)

This brings me to a complaint that I often face from my own readers. Why is it necessary to have all this foul language and these graphic descriptions of violence? The answer is because this is how people often speak, and this is what they often do. People also have sex in ways that seem less than decorous to observers, and they go to the toilet, and they drink too much and throw up. Describing all this will not save a broken plot, but it is something that has a place in any novel that tries to put the reader into a world filled with real men and women. As for the further complaint that the specific words used may be anachronistic, and may sound more like Ray

Winstone than the men whose smooth, marble busts have come down to us from classical Antiquity—well, the answer is obvious. The convention is that what the author writes is a good translation into English from the original Greek. It would never do to have a character say: "A light came on in my head," or "The temperature was dropping fast." These are phrases that could only be used in a technological civilisation. But anything else, no matter how vulgar, is fair game for an historical novelist.

Oh, and there is also this, from Jahiz, an Arab writer of the ninth century:

> Some people who affect asceticism and self denial are uneasy and embarrassed when cunt, cock and fucking are mentioned. But most men you find like that are without knowledge, honour, nobility or dignity.

What more to say? Well, I could say that I am jealous of Jack's choice of period. My choice of early Byzantium is a good one. Contrary to the general view, this was an age of heroism and genius. The fight the Byzantines put up against the barbarians and Persians and Moslems saved Western civilisation. There are few stories more inspiring than the defeat of the Arabs outside the very walls of Constantinople in 678 and 717. At the same time, nothing compares with what the Athenians achieved a thousand years earlier.

Forget the Egyptians and the Jews. Forget what we are told about the ancient Indians and Chinese. Forget even the Romans. Between about 600 and 300 BC, the Greeks of Athens and some of the cities of what is now the Turkish coast were easily the most remarkable people who ever lived. They gave us virtually all our philosophy, and the foundation of all our sciences. Their historians were the finest. Their poetry was second only to that of Homer—and it was they who put together all that we have of Homer. They gave us ideals of beauty, the fading of which has always been a warning sign of decadence; and they gave us the technical means of recording that beauty. They had no examples to imitate. They did everything entirely by themselves. In a world that had always been at the midnight point of barbarism and superstition, they went off like a flashbulb; and everything good in our own world is part of their afterglow. Every renaissance and enlightenment we have had since then has begun with a rediscovery of the ancient Greeks. Modern chauvinists may argue whether England or France or Germany has given more to the world. In truth, none of us is fit to kiss the dust on which the ancient Greeks walked.

This is the world that Luke and Hal do their bit to save. The Greeks had to win at Marathon. They had to win at Salamis and Plataia. Anything else would have condemned humanity to more of the same. Everything I was brought up to think had been achieved at Trafalgar or the Battle of Britain really was achieved in those three battles. It is the most inspiring story that can be told. You need to be a wretched novelist not to catch something of its universal importance. And Jack England is a very fine novelist. He does not denigrate the Persians—Datis is a most interesting and even sympathetic character. Nor, as shown, does he fail to recognise the brutality of the Greeks. At the same time, he knows which side he is on in the war for civilisation.

So buy this book. Buy many copes, and given them to your friends and loved ones. And let us hope that the next instalment in Luke's mission to save the human race will not be long delayed.

Review Article, Heraclius: Emperor of Byzantium

Heraclius:Emperor of Byzantium
Walter E. Kaegi
Cambridge University Press, 2003, 380pp
ISBN 0 521 81459 6

This is the first biography of Heraclius in over a century, and the first ever in English. That a biography was worth writing should be clear from the book's cover note:

> This book evaluates the life and times of the pivotal yet controversial and poorly understood Byzantine Emperor Heraclius (AD 610-641), a contemporary of the Prophet Muhammad. Heraclius' reign is critical for understanding the background to fundamental changes in the Balkans and the Middle East, including the emergence of Islam, at the end of Antiquity.

Though few in England know of him, Heraclius is one of the most astonishing figures in history. Except they are true, the facts of his life read like something out of legend. He seized power in 610 just as the Persians were turning their war with the Empire from a set of opportunistic raids into an attempt at its destruction. During the next ten years, every Imperial frontier crumbled. After a thousand years of control by Greeks, or by Greeks and Romans, Persia and Egypt fell to the Persians.. The Slavs and Avars took most of Greece. The Lombards and Visigoths nibbled away at the remaining European provinces in the West. Africa aside, the Empire was reduced to a core that covered roughly the same area as modern Turkey.

Suddenly, after a decade of seeming inactivity, Heraclius went on the offensive and struck deep inside the

Persian Empire. In a series of brilliant campaigns, he shattered the Persians and won everything back. In 629, he went in triumph to Jerusalem and restored the fragment of the True Cross that had been taken by the Persians. It seemed to be the start of a new age of Roman greatness, in which its absolutely triumphant Emperor— the new Alexander—could remake the world as he pleased.

Five years later, and without warning, the Moslems streamed out of the desert and took Syria. Another few years, and they took Egypt. By the time he died, Heraclius had lost nearly every one of the regained territories. And these were now permanently lost. From the ashes of the Eastern Roman Empire would emerge the Byzantine state and society in much the same form as they preserved down to 1204.

You can hardly go wrong in telling the story. Gibbon did it well. So did Finlay. So did Oman. So did many in the twentieth century. I have now written six novels set in seventh century Byzantium, and you really have to work hard not to convey something of how remarkable the age was. Yet, for all his undoubted mastery of the sources in at least four languages, Walter E. Kaegi makes an embarrassingly good effort at draining all sense of wonder from the story.

First, there is the writing of the book. It begins well enough—even if the discussion of possible Armenian origins soon outstays its welcome. After a few dozen pages, though, the narrative breaks down into a mass of repetitions. Look at this:

> Both antagonists remained on the battlefield after the combat. Byzantine cavalrymen watered their horses to arrow-shots' distance from the Persian horsemen, who watched over their dead until the seventh hour of the night. (p.162)

> At the end of the battle of Nineveh, after the stripping of the dead, and while the Zoroastrian Persians

> watched over their dead for a minimal observance of respect, the Byzantines, at a distance of two arrow-shots (approximately 266 or 600 meters), watered and fed their horses. (p.163)

> After defeat, the Persians, in what was a kind of standoff, having lost 6,000 men, kept a watch over the corpses of their dead..., following Zoroastrian strictures, but for a more limited duration, for one-fifth or so of a day (probably an abbreviated watch for military exingencies). (p.169)

These repetitions are carried to the point where I suspect that Professor Kaegi, over many years, jotted his thoughts onto postcards, and wrote his book by arranging the cards into loose order and not revising anything at all. Apart from looking incompetent, he manages to ruin any sense of narrative.

Then we have continual assertions of what might have been, but for which we have little or no evidence. For example:

> Heraclius probably used the threat of abandoning Constantinople for Africa to help persuade the Patriarch Sergios and the clergy and the Constantinopolitan public to accept, or be resigned to, the forced loan of ecclesiastical plate and to accept other extraordinary governmental measures. (p.111)

This might have happened. There is nothing wrong with asking what might have been in history. I do this all the time in my novels. I see no reason why historians should refuse to speculate. For Professor Kaegi, however, it seems to have crowded out many things that should have gone into his book.

He does not give a clear overview of the Orthodox and Monophysite dispute about the nature of Christ. Nor does he show how the Monothelite compromise was an attempt at shutting down almost two centuries of rancorous debate. The omission is a grave fault, as there was no boundary in this age between religion and politics. Possibly one reason why Syria and Egypt fell so easily once the Persians broke through the frontiers was that the Semites largely believed in a single nature for Christ and the Greeks did not. Each side saw the other as heretical. This may also have allowed a shared outlook with the Arabs when they invaded. Why Greek hegemony collapsed so easily in Syria and Egypt cannot be explained by any single cause. But religion was one of the important causes.

Again, there is no systematic or ultimately meaningful discussion of how the Empire twice managed to survive the loss of Syria and Egypt. These had always been rich territories, contributing much in taxes and manpower. And Egypt, for over six hundred years, had been sending around seven million bushels of corn every year, first to Rome, then to Constantinople. The corn was sold or given to the people. It fed armies on campaign. It was handed out as bribes to allies or enemies. How did the Empire get over this loss? What effect might it have had on the population of Constantinople? How far might the numbers have declined? To what extent might the Imperial capital have become less parasitic?

Above all perhaps, there is the brief mention of an anomaly that I have long wondered about, but no discussion of how this might transform our understanding of Byzantium during and after the reign of Heraclius. Back in the third century, the undivided Empire had faced increased pressure on two fronts—the arrival of the Goths on the Rhine and Danube, and the Persian revival in the East. By and large, the frontiers were held. But there was a fiscal crisis that led to debasement of the silver coinage. Though the frontiers simply collapsed after 602, the gold coinage was not debased. Indeed, in 615—between the loss of Syria and of Egypt—the silver coinage was stabilised for the first time, and the new standard lasted for centuries. What was going on? The established narrative is one of catastrophic decline, only briefly arrested, and only finally overcome by internal recovery and the decay of Islamic power. But hard money has no place in this narrative. Professor Kaegi writes much about forced loans of plate from the Church, and secular confiscations. But I do not see how these could account for a bi-metallic stability that lasted though all the interlocking crises of the seventh century and beyond.

Now, my credentials for announcing new theories are slight. I am a novelist. I have not spent a lifetime studying Byzantium in a university. On the other hand, I am reasonably competent in the two classical languages, and have read all the Greek and Latin literary sources, either in the original or in translation. I have read my way through most of the Dumbarton Oaks conference papers, and dozens of other journal articles. I have read many of the relevant archaeological reports, and the main overviews of the numismatic and epigraphic sources. In saying what I think, I have some right to a hearing.

I suspect is that the seventh century was far less disastrous than the subsequent historians have claimed. The real collapse happened in the middle of the sixth century, when bubonic plague killed over a third of the Mediterranean population. It was now that Syria and Egypt lost their Greek elites, and ceased to contribute anything meaningful to the Empire. They remained attached only so long as no other power was able to detach them. The Empire itself retreated into its "Turkish" core. Within this, a largely Greek and mostly Orthodox population slowly recovered. It was barely touched by the Persian and Arab wars, and was always able to provide sufficient armies and taxes to defend the core. Syria and Egypt could be recovered from the Persians because they were overstretched, and Heraclius was clever enough in the end to defeat them inside Persia with minimal forces. Recovering territory from the Arabs was another matter—but the Arabs never broke for long into the core.

If we assume that the mediaeval Byzantine Empire had already come into being by the time Justinian died in 565, the reverses of the next century were less a disaster than somewhere between an embarrassment and a blessing. Perhaps the currency was never debased because no one in government was that concerned about the lost territories.

But let me return to the book in question. It would have been useful had it contained a discussion of the decay of Latin in the Empire, and its replacement by Greek as the official language. Professor Kaegi does mention the change in the Imperial titles from something long and pompous and very Roman to the simple *Pisteuos en Christo Basileus*. But there is no sense here of how one civilisation is giving way to another. George of Pisidia is used as a source. But we are not told that he wrote his epic in iambic trimeter rather than the traditional hexameters. That would have led us into the interesting matter of how Greek was spoken in the seventh century, and the relationship between the living and the increasingly distant exemplars on whom they tried to base themselves. I suppose you can find all this in Warren Treadgold. You can certainly find it in the Dumbarton Oaks papers. But a biography of Heraclius without any of the cultural background is of doubtful value.

To be fair, the book does have its good points. There are excellent notes and a comprehensive bibliography. Also, Professor Kaegi tells me things about the campaigns in Persia that I did not know. He locates and describes the battlefields. No one else has done this. Also, I had supposed that Heraclius won annihilating victories. In fact, he won a series of what amount to skirmishes, relying on diplomacy and the terror of his name to bring an already exhausted Persia crumbling into dust. And, better than anyone else has, this explains why he failed to stop the Arabs. Unlike the Persians, they needed annihilating defeats that were not possible given the resources available. Or their generals needed to be bribed or tricked into treason against the Caliph in ways that the fellowship of early Islamic civilisation made impossible. If you persist with this book, you will not come away empty handed.

On the whole, however, the book is disappointing. It could have been so much better. Perhaps it will be—if only it can be rewritten for a second edition.

Review Article, *Myth and History*

Myth and History
Stephen James Yeates
Oxbow Books, Oxford, 2012, 496pp, £29.95 (pbk)
ISBN-13: 978-1842174784

I was told about this book by Dararis Tighe, whose own review can be found on Amazon. I refer you to her comments on its poor writing and sloppy editing. These are entirely just. Instead of repeating her, though, I will concentrate on the substantive claims made in the book. These are summarised in the product description:

> Our recent understanding of British history has been slowly unravelling thanks to new techniques such as DNA analysis, new archaeological data and reassessment of the literary evidence. There are considerable problems in understanding the early history of Britain; sources for the centuries from the first Roman invasion to 1000 AD are few and contradictory, the archaeological record complex and there is little collaboration or agreement between archaeologists, Roman and Anglo-Saxon historians. A common assumption concerning the development of the English language and, therefore British history, is that there was an invasion from northern Europe in the fifth century, the so-called Anglo-Saxon migration; a model based on the writings of Bede. However the Bedan model has become increasingly unsustainable and is on the verge of collapse. Myth and History offers a comprehensive re-assessment of the present scientific, historical, archaeological and language evidence, debunking the model of British history based on Bede, and showing how Roman texts can be used in conjunction with the other evidence to build an alternative picture. Stephen Yeates demonstrates that the evidence that has been used to construct the story of an Anglo-Saxon migration, with an incoming

population replacing most, if not all, of the British population has been found wanting, that initial attempts to interpret literally the DNA evidence based on historical sources are problematic, and that the best DNA analysis of the British Isles fits the evidence into a broader European view which attempts to plot the movement of people across the Continent and which sees the major migration periods in Europe as occurring in the Mesolithic and the Neolithic. This DNA analysis is constant with the latest assessments based on language development, contemporary historical reports from the Roman period, and the analysis of archaeological data from the Iron Age and Roman period. He also argues that the Roman texts can be used to identify where the Late Roman provinces of Britain actually lay and this leads to important conclusions about the ethnicity and origins of the early British peoples. This book is a timely attempt to unravel myth from history, present a cogent platform for Anglo-Saxon studies and understand who the British people really are.

In short, Dr Yeates claims a history for the English people and the English language that begins on this island long before the fifth century and that was merely overlain for a while by the Roman conquest of the first century. His approach is similar to that taken by the Whig constitutional historians of the seventeenth century. It was essential for their response to the demands of the Stuart Kings to show that there had been no break in the continuity of our history, and that the rights they were defending had emerged from the mist of time, coterminous with, or even prior to, the Monarchy itself. I will not speculate on whether Dr Yeates has an underlying agenda—though I might be in sympathy with it. I only say that I find his claim unlikely.

Antiquity ended in Western Europe during the fourth and fifth centuries. At the beginning of this transformation, the whole of Europe, from the southern banks of the Rhine onward, was part of a single Empire, ruled from Rome or Constantinople or Ravenna. At the end, it was a set of barbarian kingdoms. This formal change was accompanied by a shrinkage of population and trade that ended the urban civilisation created and sustained by Imperial rule.

In Continental Europe, however, the transformation was not total. Christianity survived. Latin remained the language of the common people, and of law and administration. Though their populations fell greatly—even in Rome, from about a million to perhaps thirty thousand—the cities were mostly not abandoned, and they tended to keep their Roman names. The civilisation of Antiquity declined, but never wholly fell. In time, the barbarian rulers were assimilated in language and faith to their subjects, and the new civilisation that emerged retained many continuities with the old.

The common sense evidence suggests that it was different in what became England. The British provinces of the Empire were often heavily Romanised. London may have been the third largest city in the Western Empire, after Rome and Carthage. The countryside was dotted with opulent villas. Christianity was the established faith, and the British Church sent bishops to the Councils of Nicaea and of Rimini, among others. Latin was used for all written purposes, from inscriptions to graffiti.

By the sixth century, Roman civilisation was ended in Britain. Christianity did not vanish, but the new rulers were pagans. The English had to be reconverted, from the end of the century, by a fresh mission from Rome. The cities appear to have been abandoned for several hundred years. When rebuilt, it was always with different street patterns, and usually with different names. Very few Roman structures, other than the usefully defensive, survived into the mediaeval period. Latin disappeared from common use. It was reintroduced by the Church, but the language of law and administration was English. Indeed, the earliest vernacular literature in Western Europe is in English.

The only exceptions can be found in those areas of

Roman Britain where the majority spoke a Celtic language. Here, Christianity remained the faith of the people. Here, some knowledge of Latin remained.

From this, we can reasonably assume a much more radical break on this island than elsewhere in the Western Empire. On the Continent, the barbarians settled among the natives, and assimilated. In England, there seems to have been some degree of replacement. If we had no literary evidence, it would be reasonable to assume an invasion and conquest, and a mass-settlement of outsiders.

But we do have literary evidence. We have the writings of Gildas and of Bede. The first was a Celtic monk, who seems to have lived through the invasion. The second wrote a few generations after the newcomers had been converted to Christianity. They wrote from opposite sides in the battle for this island. They both positively assert what the evidence suggests.

Of course, no historical text can be taken for granted. Just because something is written does not make it true. This being said, there are some common sense rules of evidence we can apply to historical statements, to distinguish what is probably false from what may be true.

First, we ask if an alleged statement is inherently unlikely. The resurrections from the dead and other miracles recorded in religious history can be largely dismissed. In some cases, they may have an alternative natural explanation: perhaps someone was not dead after all. Mostly, they are claims that, if true, would overturn our experience of the world as a place governed by natural and invariable relationships of events. For example, Bede records that, when St Alban was martyred, a well miraculously appeared where his severed head stopped rolling. I find this an unlikely claim.

I grant that historians have often rejected facts that we know to be true, when they were inconsistent with what was believed at the time about the world. Herodotus records the claim of someone who sailed round Africa that, the sun at midday was to the north. He takes this as evidence that the claim was false. But we know more about the world than Herodotus did. We have better grounds for distinguishing between the marvellous and the probable. This is not to say that miracles do not happen—only that there must be a strong presumption against specific interventions by God.

Second—and this is similar in its nature to the above—we ask if historical claims are supported or contradicted by archaeological or other evidence. For example, Herodotus says that Xerxes led an army of three million men into Greece. This is an unlikely claim. Armies that size were unknown till the twentieth century, because they could not be fed or coordinated. Looking at this and other numbers he mentions, it seems that he inflated the numbers from his Persian sources by about a thousand per cent.

Again, much of what he says about Egyptian history is not supported by our own reading of the Egyptian sources, or by the archaeological evidence—though it may tell us what foreign tourists in Egypt were told when Herodotus was writing.

Third, we ask if a writer has an interest in making a particular claim. For example, ecclesiastical historians have an interest in alleging miracles, and also in blackening the reputations of their opponents. Again, Soviet historians had an interest in blaming the Germans for every atrocity committed in Eastern Europe during the Second World War—including those, like the Katyn Wood massacre, that were committed by the Soviets. Finding that an historian has an interest that may override his duty to the truth does not invalidate anything he says, but should make us cautious about accepting any claim unsupported by good outside evidence.

Fourth, we ask if the truth of what a man says about contemporary or semi-contemporary events is likely to be known by his contemporaries. We know that a powerful State can sometimes impose falsehoods, so that they are accepted even by those who would otherwise know better. But States with this degree of power are a modern development. An historian may fill his narrative with accounts of miracles and with self-serving falsehoods. But he will probably not make incidental claims that are scandalously false, and that no one else has any obvious reason to make himself believe against all the other evidence. For example, Cicero says many things against Mark Antony that may not be true. But he does not claim that he was a hunchback, or a coward, or that he had been replaced by Cleopatra with an imposter. He does not say that Gaius Verres was illegitimate or a barbarian immigrant.

There are other tests that we can apply to claims about the past. But these will do. Strip out all the miracles, and there is nothing improbable about the invasions described by Gildas and Bede. Their essential claims are supported by other evidence. Neither had any obvious interest in lying about the fact of the invasions. No one is known to have stood up and laughed in their faces. We say, then, that there was a movement of peoples into Britain from about the fourth century onwards; that the newcomers displaced the Romanised Britons, who thereafter lived on the fringes of the island; that the civilisation of the Anglo-Saxons was a new and alien growth. Unlike the French and Spanish and Italians, the English did not start as degraded Romans. We were a new people. We felt the influence of Rome only after we had emerged into history.

Against this, the DNA evidence alleged is of no value. If someone says that slitting a live pigeon open and applying it to the buboes was an effective cure for the Black Death, we have the right to be dubious. We know too much about medicine. But DNA testing is a new science. Its conclusions are often turned upside down by fresh discoveries. So far, indeed, its main use has been by the authorities to fit people up for crimes they may or may not have committed, but for which the normal evidence would not convince a jury. In its present state, DNA testing is not sufficient to overturn claims as well-attested as the English invasions of Britain at the end of Antiquity.

This being said, I feel no obligation to enter closely into the question of what language the Britons spoke. The Romans seem to have thought they spoke a sort of Celtic. Hardly anyone has doubted that since. The Welsh and Cornish speak, or spoke, Celtic languages. Looking at the names of people and places we have from the native Britons—Boadicea, Caractacus, Sulis, Camulodunum—I am not persuaded by Dr Yeates that they spoke any sort of Germanic.

Nor need I explain the details of how the native Britons were displaced, or how their descendants became the Welsh and the Cornish. Broadly speaking, though, there are two possible explanations of what happened. The first is that most of them died or were killed. Leaving aside the possibility of genocide—a regrettable, though not unusual, approach to settling who owns a territory—the sixth century was an age of pandemic diseases. These may have differentially affected the inhabitants of Britain. Perhaps the Britons had close contacts with the Mediterranean world, and the English had none. Perhaps the English settlers moved into a demographic vacuum.

Just as likely, the Britons were not killed, but conquered and converted. A thousand years ago, most people who lived in modern Turkey were Greek Christians. Today, without overwhelming demographic change, they are Turkish Moslems. In that time, people changed their religion and their language. Also without any evident change of people, Coptic lost place to Arabic in Egypt during the later middle ages. It was the same in Syria with Syriac. When Spain was conquered by the Arabs, many Christian Spaniards are known to have converted. By the end of the first century, every Italian language but Latin was extinct—including Etruscan, which had no relationship with Latin. Why should it not have been the same with Britain?

But, as said, I do not know what happened it detail. I only say that the established evidence is so general, and so internally consistent, that it will take much more than this book to change my opinion of how England began.

Conspiracies of Rome
Richard Blake
Hodder & Stoughton, London
Hardback Edition: February 2008
Paperback Edition: January 2009

368pp
ISBN: 9780340951125

Rome, 609 AD. Empire is a fading memory. Repeatedly fought over and plundered, the City is falling into ruins. Filth and rubble block the streets. Killers prowl by night. Far off, in Constantinople, the Emperor has other concerns. The Church is the one institution left intact, and is now flexing its own imperial muscle.

Enter Aelric of England: young and beautiful, sexually uninhibited, heroic, if ruthlessly violent—and hungry for the learning of a world that is dying around him. In this first of six novels, he's only here by accident. Without getting that girl pregnant, and the resulting near-miss from King Ethelbert's gelding knife, he might never have left Kent. But here Aelric is, and nothing on earth will send him back.

The question is how long he will stay on earth. A deadly brawl outside Rome sucks him straight into the high politics of Empire. There is fraud. There is pursuit. There is murder after murder. Soon, Aelric is involved in a race against time to find answers. Who is trying to kill him? Where are the letters everyone thinks he has, and what do they contain? Who is the one-eyed man? What significance to all this has the Column of Phocas, the monument just put up in the Forum to celebrate a tyrant's generosity to Holy Mother Church?

Aelric does at last get his answers. What he chooses to do with them will shape the future history of Europe and the world....

"Fascinating to read, very well written, an intriguing plot and I enjoyed it very much." Derek Jacobi, star of *I Claudius* and *Gladiator*

Terror of Constantinople
Richard Blake
Hodder & Stoughton, London
Hardback Edition: February 2009
Paperback Edition: May 2010

420pp
ISBN: 9780340951149

610AD. Invaded by Persians and barbarians, the Byzantine Empire is also tearing itself apart in civil war. Phocas, the maniacally bloodthirsty Emperor, holds Constantinople by a reign of terror. The uninvaded provinces are turning one at a time to the usurper, Heraclius.

Just as the battle for the Empire approaches its climax, Aelric of England turns up in Constantinople. Blackmailed by the Papal authorities to leave off his career of lechery and market-rigging in Rome, he thinks his job is to gather texts for a semi-comprehensible dispute over the Nature of Christ. Only gradually does he realise he is a pawn in a much larger game.

What is the eunuch Theophanes up to? Why does the Papal Legate never show himself? How many drugs can the Emperor's son-in-law take before he loses his touch for homicidal torture? Above all, why has wicked old Phocas taken Aelric under his wing?

To answer these questions, Aelric has nothing on his side but beauty, charm, intellectual brilliance and a talent for cold and ruthless violence.

"[Blake's] plotting can seem off-puttingly anarchic until the penny drops that everyone is simultaneously embroiled in multiple, often conflicting, scams. Aelric's survival among the last knockings of empire in Constantinople depends not on deducing who wants him dead, but who wants him dead at any given moment." *The Daily Telegraph*

Blood of Alexandria
Richard Blake
Hodder & Stoughton, London
Hardback Edition: June 2010
Paperback Edition: February 2011
502pp
ISBN: 978-0340951163

The tears of Alexander shall flow, giving bread and freedom
. . .

612 AD. Egypt, the jewel of the Roman Empire, seethes
with unrest, as bread runs short and the Persians plot an invasion. In Alexandria, a city divided between Greeks and Egyptians by language, religion and far too few soldiers, the
mummy of the Great Alexander, dead for nine hundred years,
still has the power to calm the mob—or inflame it . . .

In this third novel of the series, Aelric of England has become the Lord Senator Alaric and the trusted Legate of the
Emperor Heraclius. He's now in Alexandria, to send Egypt's
harvest to Constantinople, and to force the unwilling Viceroy
to give land to the peasants. But the city—with its factions and
conspirators—thwarts him at every turn. And when an old
enemy from Constantinople arrives, supposedly on a quest for
a religious relic that could turn the course of the Persian war,
he will have to use all his cunning, his charm and his talent for
violence to survive.

"As always, Blake writes with immense historical and classical erudition, while displaying an ability to render 1500-
year-old conversations in realistically colloquial English." *C4SS*

Sword of Damascus
Richard Blake
Hodder & Stoughton, London
Hardback Edition: June 2011
Paperback Edition: January 2012
432pp
ISBN: 978-1444709667

687 AD. Expansive and triumphant, the Caliphate has
stripped Egypt and Syria from the Byzantine Empire. Farther
and farther back, the formerly hegemonic Empire has been
pushed—once to the very walls of its capital, Constantinople.

All that has saved it from destruction is the invention of
Greek Fire. Is it a liquid? Is it a gas? Is it a gift from God or
the Devil? Or is it a recipe found in an ancient tomb? Few
know the answer. But all know how it has broken the Islamic
advance and restored Byzantine control of the seas.

Yes, without this "miracle weapon," Constantinople would
have fallen in the 7th century, rather than the 15th, and the
new barbarian kingdoms of Europe would have gone down
one by one before the unstoppable cry of *Allah al akbar!*

But what importance has all this to old Aelric, now in his
nineties, and a refugee from the Empire he's spent his life
holding together? No longer the Lord Senator Alaric, Brother
Aelric is writing his memoirs in the remote wastes of northern
England, and waiting patiently for death. For company, he has
his student, Wilfred, sickly through bright, and Brother Jo-
seph, another refugee from the Empire. Or there's ghastly
Brother Cuthbert to despise—or to envy for his possession of
pretty young Edward.

Then a band of northern barbarians turns up outside the
monastery—and then another. Almost before he can draw
breath, Aelric is a prisoner and, with Edward, headed straight
back into the snake pit of Mediterranean rivalries.

Who has snatched Aelric out of retirement, and why? What
is the nature of Edward's fascination with a man more than
eighty years his senior? How, together, will they handle the
confrontation that lies at the end of their journey—a confrontation that will settle the future of mankind?

Will age have robbed Aelric of his charm, his intelligence,

his resourcefulness, or of his talent for cold and homicidal duplicity?

"As always, Blake's plotting is as brilliantly devious as the mind of his sardonic and very earthy hero. This is a story of villainy that reels you in from its prosaic opening through a series of death-defying thrills and spills." *The Lancashire Evening Post*

Ghosts of Athens
Richard Blake
Hodder & Stoughton, London
Paperback Edition: April 2013
448pp
ISBN: 9781444709704

612 AD. No longer the glorious cradle of all art and science, Athens is a ruined provincial city in one of the Byzantine Empire's less vital provinces. Why, then, has the Emperor diverted Aelric's ship home from Egypt to send him here? Why has he included Priscus in the warrant? Surely, they have more important business in Constantinople. Isn't Aelric needed to save the Empire's finances, and Priscus to lead its armies against the Persians? Or has the Emperor decided to blame them for the bloodbath they presided over in Egypt?

Or could it be that Aelric's latest job just to manage a council of Eastern and Western Bishops more inclined to kick each other to death than agree to a wildly controversial position on the Nature of Christ?

Hard to say. Impossible to say. When did Heraclius ever explain his reasons—assuming he had any in the first place? The only certainty is that Aelric finds himself in a derelict palace of dark and endless corridors and of rooms that Martin, his cowardly secretary, assures him pulse with an ancient evil.

Add to this a headless corpse, drained of its blood, a bizarre cult of the self-emasculated, embezzlement, a city rabble on the edge of revolution—and the approach of an army rumoured to contain twenty million starving barbarians.

Is Aelric on a high level mission to save the Empire? Or has he been set up to fail? Or is the truth even worse than he can at first imagine?

This fifth novel in the series blends historical fiction with gothic horror. Not surprisingly, Aelric may find even the vile Priscus a welcome ally. Or perhaps he won't....

"It would be hard to over-praise this extraordinary series, a near-perfect blend of historical detail and atmosphere with the plot of a conspiracy thriller, vivid characters, high philosophy and vulgar comedy." *The Morning Star*

Curse of Babylon
Richard Blake
Hodder & Stoughton, London
Paperback Edition: August 2013
496pp
ISBN: 9781444709735

615 AD. A vengeful Persian tyrant prepares the final blow that will annihilate the Byzantine Empire.

Aelric of England—now the Lord Senator Alaric—is almost as powerful as the Emperor. Seemingly without opposition, he dominates the vast and morally bankrupt city of Constantinople. If, within his fortified palace, he revels in his books, his mood-altering substances, and the various delights of his serving girls and dancing boys, he alone is able to conceive and to push forward reforms that are the Empire's only hope of survival, and perhaps of restoration to wealth and greatness.

But his domestic enemies are waiting for their moment to strike back. And the world's most terrifying military machine is assembling in secret beyond the mountains of the eastern frontier.

What is the Horn of Babylon? Is it really accursed? Who is Antonia? What is Shahin, the bestial Persian admiral, doing on a ship within sight of the Imperial City? What exactly does Chosroes, the still more bestial Great King of Persia, want from Aelric? Is Rado a thuggish dancing boy or a military genius? Will Priscus, the vile and disgraced former Commander of the East, get his place in the history books? Must it be written in Aelric's blood?

In this sixth novel in the series, can Aelric rise to his greatest challenge yet—and find a personal happiness that has so far eluded him?

Intrigue, sex, black comedy, spectacular crowd scenes and extreme violence—you will find it all here in luxuriant abundance.

"[Blake] knows how to deliver a fast-paced story and his grasp of the period is impressively detailed" *Mail on Sunday*

The Churchill Memorandum
Sean Gabb
Hampden Press, London, 2014
ISBN: 9781311160829

A thriller in the style of John Buchan and Sapper and the early Ian Fleming, *The Churchill Memorandum* presents an exciting alternative history of the twentieth century.

Imagine a world in which Hitler died in 1939. No World War II. No US-Soviet duopoly of the world. No slide into the gutter for England.

Anthony Markham doesn't need to imagine. It is now 1959, and this is the only world he knows. England is still England. The Queen-Empress is on her throne. The pound is worth a pound. Lord Halifax is Prime Minister, and C.S. Lewis is Archbishop of Canterbury. All is right with the world—or with that quarter of it lucky enough to repose under an English heaven.

Not surprisingly, Markham loves England. He worships England. Never mind that he's Indian on his mother's side, and not entirely as he'd like to be seen in one other respect: he keeps these little faults hidden—oh, *very* well hidden!

Now, twenty years after Hitler's death in a car accident, he is taking leave of a nightmarish, totalitarian America. He has a biography to write of a dead and largely forgotten Winston Churchill, and has had to travel to where the old drunk left his papers. But little does he realise, as he returns to his safe, orderly England, that he carries, somewhere in his luggage, an object that can be used to destroy England and the whole structure of bourgeois civilisation as it has been gradually restored since 1918.

Who is trying to kill Anthony Markham? For whom is Major Stanhope really working? Where did Dr Pakeshi get his bag of money? Is there a connection between Michael Foot, Leader of the British Communist Party, and Foreign Secretary Harold Macmillan? Why is Ayn Rand in an American prison, and Nathaniel Branden living in a South London bedsit? Why is Alan Greenspan dragged off and shot in the first chapter? Where does Enoch Powell fit into the story?

Above all, what is the Churchill Memorandum? What terrible secrets does it contain?

All will be revealed—but not till after Markham has gone on the run through an England unbombed, uncentralised, still free, and still mysterious.

How might our country have turned out but for that catastrophic declaration of war in defence of Poland? Read on and wonder....

The Churchill Memorandum is a thriller, a black comedy and a satire. It is the first novel in Sean Gabb's "England Trilogy."

The Break
Sean Gabb
Hampden Press, London, 2014
ISBN: 9781310247996

In this second part of his "England Trilogy," Sean Gabb leaves alternative history for dystopian fantasy.

No one knows what caused The Break eleven months ago, but there's no sign of its end.

England is settling into its new future as a reindustrialising concentration camp. The rest of the world is watching... waiting... curious...

It's Wednesday the 7th March 2018 – in the mainland UK. Everywhere else, it's some time in June 1065.

Jennifer thinks her family survived The Hunger because of their smuggling business – tampons and paracetamol to France, silver back to England. Little does she know what game her father was really playing, as she recrosses the Channel from an impromptu mission of her own. Little can she know how her life has already been torn apart.

Who has taken Jennifer's parents? Where are they? What is the Home Secretary up to with the Americans? Why is she so desperate to lay hands on Michael? Will Jesus Christ return to Earth above Oxford Circus? When will the "Doomsday Project" go live?

Can the Byzantine Empire and the Catholic Church take on the British State, and win?

All will be answered – if Jennifer can stay alive in a post-apocalyptic London terrorised by hunger, by thugs in uniform, and by motorbike gangs of Islamic suicide bombers.

The York Deviation
Sean Gabb
Hampden Press, London, 2014
ISBN: (Forthcoming)

Edward Parker is getting old. He's overweight. His knees are going. So are his teeth. His career as a barrister has been mediocre at best. Family aside, his main outside interest lies in libertarian politics. All this has given him is a ringside seat for watching England's descent into a grotty police state, riddled with political correctness and police brutality.

Oh, but there's also his dream life. This is vivid and spectacular in all the ways that real life isn't. In particular, the dreams he's been having since childhood of a primaeval city, inhabited by reptilian bipeds, are almost a second life.

Then he opens his eyes into his most vivid and spectacular dream of all. He's an undergraduate again at the University of York. It's Monday, the 16th February 1981. In great things and in little, everything seems at first exactly as it had been.

Only it isn't.

As the dream unfolds, and shows no appearance of ending, deviation after deviation from the remembered past accumulate, and settle into the appearance of a coherent narrative. But where is this taking young Edward Parker? What is his old "friend" Cruttling up to? Where have all his real friends gone? What secret lurks in the vast Temple of Isis being uncovered behind the main library? Why is Professor Fairburn so desperate to lay hands on that secret? Will Margaret Thatcher get what she wants?

Above all, what do other dreams keep bleeding into this one?

Or is this a dream? If it isn't what does it mean for and England not yet in the gutter, but only hovering on the kerb?

In this concluding part of his "England Trilogy," Sean Gabb leaves both alternative history and dystopian fantasy. *The York Deviation* is a novel about second chances—second chances for its narrator, and perhaps for England too.

CPSIA information can be obtained at www.ICGtesting.com
Printed in the USA
LVOW04s2017211214

419840LV00022B/569/P